# CAPTIVATE YOUR READERS

## An Editor's Guide to Writing Compelling Fiction

## Jodie Renner

Captivate Your Readers – An Editor's Guide to Writing Compelling Fiction

Author: Jodie Renner

Published by Cobalt Books, www.CobaltBooks.net, Kelowna, B.C., Canada

ISBN: 978-0993700415

Library and Archives Canada Cataloguing in Publication:

Renner, Jodie, author

Captivate your readers : an editor's guide to writing compelling fiction / Jodie Renner.

Includes bibliographical references.

ISBN 978-0-9937004-1-5 (pbk.)

1. Fiction--Authorship. 2. Fiction--Technique. I. Title.

PN3355.R455 2015    808.3        C2015-901911-7

Cover Design by Travis Miles, www.ProBookCovers.com

# Praise for Captivate Your Readers
# – An Editor's Guide to Writing Compelling Fiction

"A handy compendium of techniques that will also serve as a checklist for authors who aspire to write page-turning fiction."
– **James Scott Bell**, author of *Super Structure: The Key to Unlocking the Power of Story*

"Jodie Renner's books are packed with practical writing and editing advice. Get ready to improve your manuscript today."
– **Steven James**, author of *Story Trumps Structure: How to Write Unforgettable Fiction by Breaking the Rules*

"Want to write solid, marketable fiction? Read this book. Regardless of your experience level, *Captivate Your Readers* gives you clear and concise tools that will help you create a believable story world and spin a good yarn."
– **DP Lyle**, award-winning author of the Dub Walker and Samantha Cody thriller series

"Jodie Renner nails it! *Captivate Your Readers* should be at the top of every new and experienced writer's arsenal, as well as a preferred resource for every teacher of writing. Her no-nonsense, easy-to-understand approach is perfect. Bravo, Jodie Renner!"
– **Lynn Sholes**, bestselling author of the Cotten Stone series and *The Shield*

"Jodie Renner is a terrific editor and writing coach. I highly recommend all of her books."
– **L.J. Sellers**, bestselling thriller writer

"I couldn't put this book down! A writing and editing book that's both educational and entertaining. *Captivate Your Readers* is my newest go-to writing resource."

– **Mark Wayne Adams**, President, FAPA; CEO, MWA, Inc.

"Step by step, chapter by chapter, Jodie examines and clarifies what readers want these days, how to make it happen, and – more importantly – how to add your own spin to her lessons and craft a compelling story the reader cannot put down."

– **William Simon**, writer

"From character development, to hooking the reader with your opening, to showing nail-biting detail, to immersing the reader in the story world, to sparking up your style, this book will help you keep the reader reading."

– **Steve Hooley**, writer

"The book made me stop again and again. It made me contemplate and brainstorm on my work in progress. Every time I had a light-bulb experience (and there were plenty of them) I had an urge to apply this to my work. Which I did. I am sure to come back to this book again and again.... So, my print version will definitely get a lot of dog ears. And so will yours. Guaranteed."

– **Victoria Ichizli-Bartels**, writer

"This book is a winner. I found the writing craft recommendations on target with lots of excellent examples. The reader-friendly format and insightful content make it a great instructional read as well as a tool to reach for whenever one's writing is feeling 'off'. Highly recommended."

– **Tom Combs**, author of medical thriller *Nerve Damage*

# TABLE OF CONTENTS

## PART V – IMMERSE THE READERS IN YOUR STORY WORLD

## PART VI – SPARK UP YOUR STYLE AND ADD TENSION & INTRIGUE

## PART VII – OVERVIEW, CHECKLISTS, ADDITIONAL TIPS

## APPENDICES

# Introduction

Are you looking for techniques to bring your fiction to life for the readers so they feel they're right there, on the edge of their seats, struggling with the hero or heroine? Staying up late at night, worrying, glued to the pages?

This guide provides specific advice, with examples, for captivating readers and immersing them in your story world.

It's all about providing a direct connection between the characters and the readers through techniques such as deep point of view, showing instead of telling, avoiding author intrusions, creating dialogue that zings, and basically letting the characters tell the story.

Today's readers want to put aside their cares and chores and lose themselves in an absorbing story. This book shows you how to provide the emotional involvement and immediacy readers crave in fiction.

You'll find techniques for making sure your characters come to life and your readers feel directly connected to them, without the author's hand appearing as an intermediary.

And like my other writing guides, which are all designed for busy writers, the format of this one is reader-friendly, with text broken up by subheadings, examples, and lists. Each chapter is designed to stand alone, so they can be read in any order.

I hope you'll forgive occasional references to my multi-award-winning writing guide, *Fire up Your Fiction*, for additional information, as these two books complement each other perfectly to offer a variety of valuable writing advice. *Fire up Your Fiction* has been out for a few years, so many readers will already own it. If not, you can purchase the e-book for only $3.49, if you wish, or borrow the print book from the library.

# PART I

# CREATE CHARACTERS READERS WILL WANT TO FOLLOW

# Chapter 1 – Create a Complex, Charismatic Main Character

"The first thing that makes a reader read a book is the characters." ~ John Gardner

Your novel can have an intriguing premise and riveting plot, but if your lead character is bland, wimpy, ditzy, arrogant, or lacking in personality and drive, readers won't warm up to him or care what happens to him, so they'll put the book down. Conversely, if your protagonist is fascinating, sympathetic, and clever, but complicated, readers will be drawn to him and start worrying about him, which is exactly what you want. A worried reader is an engaged reader.

"Living, vibrating human beings are still the secret and magic formula of great and enduring fiction." ~ Lajos Egri

Unsuccessful authors very often have written a promising story, but have neglected to develop their characters sufficiently. You should spend as much or more time creating depth for your lead character and learning about her strengths and weaknesses, her fears, secrets, regrets, hopes, motivations, needs, and desires as you do on creating an exciting plot.

As Elizabeth Lyon points out in *A Writer's Guide to Fiction*, "Characterization is the bedrock of fiction and the reason most people read it. What endures in our hearts and minds over time is the heroes, heroines, and villains. Less often do we recall their plots. The fiction writer's greatest challenge is character development."

A big mistake newbie fiction writers make is modeling their main character too much after themselves or someone they know.

3

Instead, to hook readers, create a fascinating lead character, one who is larger than life, more charismatic, braver, more determined, and also more troubled, with more secrets and inner conflict than the average person you know. Those attributes will make them appealing and worth following and cheering on for a whole story.

**Don't annoy your readers by making your main character:**

**~ Flat, superficial – a cardboard character**

To avoid a one-dimensional, boring protagonist, you'll need to create a complicated backstory for him, including his fears, regrets, insecurities, and desires, as well as his hopes, strengths and talents. Also, give him conflicting desires.

To get to know your character's deepest secrets, his hopes and fears, his weaknesses and regrets, and his wants versus his needs, try putting him on the psychiatrist's couch or journaling in his voice. Write in his secret diary every day, in free, stream-of-consciousness form – just let the ideas flow. Let the character vent his frustrations uncensored. What's his strongest desire right now? Why is he afraid he might not get it? What or who is standing in his way or frustrating him? What is he worried about? Angry about? What secret is he harboring that he hopes no one will discover? Why? Let the character vent here.

Also, in the actual story, a sure-fire way to deepen your character and your readers' engagement is to have him react more to events. Show how he's feeling, through his thoughts and his emotional, physical, and sensory reactions, as well as his words and actions. An emotionally flat character will leave readers cold, and they'll start thinking about what else they should be doing.

**~ Nerdy, dull – lacking in charisma or sex appeal**

As James Scott Bell says in *Revision & Self-Editing*, your lead character should have "grit, wit, and it." Grit is courage, determination, and resourcefulness. Wit, the ability to make the occasional witty or humorous comment, can rescue a character from maudlin self-pity or a moment from being overly sentimental or sappy. Wit also refers to cleverness, the ability to solve problems and think quickly in sticky situations. And "it," according to Bell, means "personal magnetism – sex appeal as well as a quality that invites admiration (or envy) among others. Someone who walks into a room and draws all the attention has 'It.'"

So be sure to make your protagonist charismatic, with lots of personality and sex appeal – and plenty of attitude.

## ~ Too wimpy, too whiny, too victimized

Don't have a primary character who's fearful about everything, who's always reacting rather than acting, who just takes what's dished out to her. Or one who's victimized, who doesn't rise to the challenge or fight back. A character who's constantly feeling sorry for herself gets tiresome quickly, and readers will lose patience with her and put the book down.

If you want your protagonist to start as a bit of a wimp, then get stronger as the story progresses, don't go on like that for too long. Make her gather her courage and wits and search for ways out of her predicament. In other words, she needs to be forced by circumstances to become stronger, more courageous, more resilient. No one wants to read about someone with a million different phobias or who's wallowing in self-pity or afraid to make a move to improve her life. We need to see some grit, some resourcefulness, some fight!

As Jack M. Bickham says in his little gem, *The 38 Most Common Fiction Writing Mistakes (And How to Avoid Them)*, "Fiction writers too often forget that interesting characters are almost always characters who are active – risk-takers – highly motivated toward a goal. Many a story has been wrecked at the outset because the writer chose to write about the wrong kind of person – a character of the type we sometimes call a wimp."

So don't model your hero or heroine after someone you know. They need to be stronger, braver, more resourceful and more intelligent,

As Jessica Page Morrell puts it in *Thanks, But This Isn't For Us*, "Fictional characters venture into physical and emotional territory where most of us would fear to tread." Readers who lead a humdrum life want to escape and vicariously live a more exciting one, through the head and heart of someone who's not afraid to challenge herself and confront her fears head-on.

On the other hand, don't go to the other extreme and make your protagonist:

### ~ Cold, unfeeling, arrogant

Your main character can and should have a few inner conflicts and character flaws, but overall, she needs to be at least somewhat sympathetic and likeable – not cold or arrogant. Your reader wants to be able to identify immediately with your lead character, to start caring about her and worrying about her. If the readers don't warm up to your protagonist and care about what happens to her within the first few pages, they'll very likely put down the book and go on to another one. If you have a tough hero with a gruff exterior, try to show some glimmers of hope, some redeeming qualities early on. Maybe show him to be sensitive or caring in some small ways, like perhaps he rescues a dog or cat in the traffic. Robert Crais does this with his gruff, strong, silent hero, Joe Pike.

Also, don't make your character:

### ~ Too perfect

A perfect character is insufferable. Don't make your hero or heroine constantly cheery, selfless and giving, stunningly beautiful or handsome, super popular, or perfectly sculpted and toned – in other words, too good to be true. Perfect people are both boring and annoying. They're boring because nothing really challenges them, so we can't identify with them; they're annoying because they don't have to work for things like the rest of us – everything's handed to them on a platter. And they're so unrealistic we think they must be faking it. And let's face it, we're probably jealous of them. You

6

want readers to identify with and bond with your protagonist, not envy them.

Nobody likes a "goody-goody two-shoes," and unless you're writing a children's story, someone who's always positive (a "Pollyanna") is annoying, too. So be sure not to make your protagonist nicer, kinder, or more selfless than your average person. Give them some character flaws, some secrets, regrets, and insecurities, a weakness or two, and maybe even a phobia.

Along the same lines, don't make your protagonist:

### ~ Too smart, too powerful

If your hero is ultra-smart and all-powerful, even big problems and challenges will be minor, a mere bump in the road. If he's not sweating or stressed or in danger, readers aren't going to worry about him. And if readers aren't worrying about the hero or heroine of the book, they aren't emotionally engaged. Which means they can put down the book at any time and look for one that engages them. So don't make your character a genius or invincible. Give him some human qualities and foibles. Even Superman could be weakened by kryptonite and was vulnerable and off-guard whenever Lois Lane was threatened. And James Bond has been done and overdone – most readers today look for a more believable, human protagonist, one they can relate to and worry about.

On the other hand, don't make your character:

### ~ Clueless or oblivious

If your protagonist is too dumb to figure out what's going on, to pick up on all or most of the clues, readers will feel like yelling at him or throwing the book across the room. Readers have no patience with a detective or other hero who's dumber than they are. They expect to meet a bright, resourceful central character, one who's worth their investment of time, one who warrants their support. If something obvious is staring your character in the face and he's not seeing it or getting it, find a way to make that info less evident, so a smart, savvy character could realistically miss it.

Similarly, don't make your character:

## ~ Ditzy, silly, or immature

Beware of airheads. They can be great for minor characters, but your hero or heroine needs to be someone readers can admire and identify with, not someone to scoff.

So when inventing your story's protagonist, be sure to make him likeable, charismatic, and complex enough to be interesting. He should be intelligent, brave, and somewhat strong, but with emotional depth and a few flaws, secrets, and insecurities or vulnerabilities. And he needs to be able to draw on inner strengths and resources to take on adversity and overcome odds. If your main character is flat, boring, perfect, arrogant, dumb, or a wimp, readers won't want to follow him for a whole story. They'll lose patience and find another book to read.

And don't make your villain 100% evil, either! He or she also needs to be multi-faceted – and intelligent, determined, and powerful – a worthy opponent for your protagonist. More on that in the next chapter.

Conflict:
) Man v. man
) " " God
) " " nature - elements, animals
) " " society
(5) Man v himself.

# Chapter 2 – Create a Fascinating, Believable Antagonist

For a riveting story, be sure to challenge your hero – or heroine – to the max. Readers need to be constantly worrying about him because his life is in upheaval and he's struggling, dealing with increasing conflict in the form of serious opposition or threats. One or more forces of opposition should threaten the protagonist or stand in the way of his goals.

Challenges don't need to be in the form of an actual character. They can be some other kind of opposing force or idea, like a fear, phobia, prejudice, or handicap that is preventing the character from reaching her goals. Perhaps her life is more challenging and frustrating due to a disability. Maybe she's sight- or hearing-impaired or wheelchair-bound. Or she suffers from anorexia or PTSD or claustrophobia, or is bipolar or obsessive-compulsive or hyperactive. Or she was sexually abused as a child.

The main threat in fiction usually comes in the form of an antagonistic character, who isn't necessarily a nasty villain. Other determined opponents include romantic rivals, "mean girls," schoolyard bullies, competing colleagues, or sports rivals. Antagonists can also fall into a gray zone of opposition characters who aren't really evil, just at odds with the protagonist we're rooting for. They can be fascinating too, as we don't know if they're going to change sides, so they're often unpredictable. One example that comes to mind is the U.S. marshal, Deputy Samuel Gerard (played by Tommy Lee Jones), who is determined to capture Harrison Ford's character, Dr. Richard Kimble, in the movie *The Fugitive*. A similar example is Sheriff Teasle in *First Blood*, who is after our hero, John Rambo. Or how about Han Solo from *Star Wars*? Not a villain, but not a good guy, either. He sparks things up though, doesn't he? Other gray characters include Rogue,

Wolverine and Gambit from *X-Men* and Q from *Star Trek*. We wonder whether these somewhat likeable or understandable bad guys could switch sides at any time.

To pose a credible, significant threat and cause readers to worry, your antagonist should be as clever, powerful, and determined as your protagonist. Challenges and troubles are what make your main character intriguing, compel her to be the best she can be. They force her to draw on resources she never knew she had in order to survive, defeat evil, or attain her goals.

For this chapter, we'll assume your antagonist is a villain – a mean, even despicable, destructive character we definitely don't want to root for. He needs to be a formidable obstacle to the protagonist's goals or a menace to the hero's loved ones or other innocents. And thrillers, fantasy, and horror require really frightening, nasty villains.

Most of the bad guys in movies and books want the same thing: power. Or maybe revenge or riches. And they don't care who gets hurt along the way. Or worse, they enjoy causing pain, even torturing their victims.

Some powerful, frightening villains in classics, modern novels, and movies include Long John Silver from *Treasure Island*, Moby-Dick, Bill Sikes from *Oliver Twist*, Mr. Hyde from *Dr. Jekyll and Mr. Hyde*, Count Dracula, Mrs. Danvers from *Rebecca*, Lex Luthor from *Superman*, the Joker from *Batman*, Max Cady from *Cape Fear*, Patrick Bateman from *American Psycho*, Darth Vader from *Star Wars*, Sauron from *The Lord of the Rings*, Jason, Freddy Krueger, and Jigsaw of horror movie fame, Voldemort from the Harry Potter books, the Wicked Witch of the West from *The Wizard of Oz*, Cruella DeVil from *The Hundred and One Dalmatians*, Ernst Stavro Blofeld from the James Bond novels, Annie Wilkes (played by Kathy Bates) from *Misery*, Mr. Smith from *The Matrix*, and Hannibal Lecter from *Red Dragon*. And of course the nonhuman monsters found in movies like *Jaws, Jurassic Park*, and *Alien*.

10

The antagonist needs to be powerful, a game-changer. As Chuck Wendig says in his excellent blog post "25 Things You Should Know About Antagonists," "The antagonist is there to push and pull the sequence of events into an arrangement that pleases him. He makes trouble for the protagonist. He is the one upping the stakes. He is the one changing the game and making it harder."

The protagonist and antagonist have clashing motivations. Their needs, values, and desires are at odds. The antagonist and protagonist could have opposite backgrounds and personalities for contrast – or be uncomfortably similar, to show how close the good guy or gal came or could come to passing over to the dark side.

Most readers are no longer intrigued by "mwoo-ha-ha," all-evil antagonists, like Captain Hook in *Peter Pan*. Unless you're writing middle-grade fiction, be sure your villain isn't inexplicably horrid – evil for the sake of evil. Today's sophisticated readers are looking for an antagonist who's more complex, realistic, and believable.

Chuck Wendig suggests antagonists should be depicted as real people with real problems: "People with wants, needs, fears, motivations. People with families and friends and their own enemies. They're full-blooded, full-bodied characters. They're not single-minded villains twirling greasy mustaches."

For a believable, fascinating antagonist or villain, try to create a unique, memorable bad guy of a type that hasn't been done to death. Give him or her an original background and voice. This is not an easy task.

Remember that the antagonist is the hero of his own story. He thinks he's right. He justifies his actions somehow, whether it's revenge, a thirst for power, ridding society of undesirables, or payback. He may even feel he has a noble or just goal, as in the serial killer of prostitutes.

To create a worthy opponent for the protagonist and a realistic, believable, complex antagonist, get into his mind-set. Ask yourself these questions:

- What does the antagonist want or need?
- Why is he determined to go after it?
- What drives the antagonist? Greed? Revenge? Hatred? Anger? Hurt?
- What is his biggest motivation? To avenge past wrongs? To gain ultimate power?
- Who does he want to suffer or lose out? Why?
- How does he justify his actions? What does he tell himself?

Now create a backstory for your antagonist. Most of it will not show up in your story, but you need to get a handle on what makes him tick to ensure he acts in ways that are in keeping with his background.

Develop his voice. As you do for the protagonist, you can write a free-form rant, where he goes on and on about why he hates someone or something, wants to get revenge, needs to find and kill certain people, and so on.

Show his justification for his goals and actions. Why does he think he's right and justified in his actions? This will create a more believable, more determined bad guy.

Perhaps identify at some point in your narrative a flashback or allusion to an experience that shows the antagonist as a victim – abused or neglected, treated cruelly by family or others in power. This can create a spark of sympathy while also potentially foreshadowing a particularly nasty incident. (Thanks to thriller author Tom Combs for this suggestion.)

Write some scenes purely from the antagonist's point of view, away from the protagonist, so readers can find out what makes him tick and how twisted he is. This also creates reader concern for the main character, which is always a good thing.

Make him scary, a force to be reckoned with, but not all-powerful, as that's unrealistic. Give him a few weaknesses, too.

And for added complexity and dimension, take it one step further by showing a human side of the antagonist, something readers can actually relate to, might be afraid they could also fall into. That amps up the tension and reader involvement.

Just as the protagonist has a character arc – her experiences change her in some way, cause her to grow internally – give the antagonist some kind of arc, too. Make him change in some way – preferably for the worse.

Chuck Wendig suggests giving the antagonist a "kick the cat" moment. It's often advised to show a tough hero's kind, caring, human side by having him save a cat or pet a dog. You can use similar imagery to highlight the cruelty of the villain. But I'd advise you not to have him actually torture or kill a dog or cat – readers really hate that!

Also, let the antagonist win and the protagonist lose a few times throughout the story to underline his frightening power and increase readers' nail-biting worry for the hero or heroine.

So to create a fascinating, believable antagonist or villain, try to make him or her unique. Delve into their background, find out the goals and motivations that drive them forward. Get into their mind and try to understand them. How do they justify their actions?

Give us a complex villain we love to hate – or a gray antagonist who makes us squirm!

# Chapter 3 – Don't Stop the Story to Introduce Each Character

## Rein in those backstory dumps.

Imagine meeting someone for the first time, and after saying hello, they go into a long monologue about their experiences growing up and their family dynamics. Then they move on to their interests, what they studied in college, jobs they've had, and why their last relationship didn't work out. Your smile is pasted to your face as you nod, then surreptitiously glance around, madly trying to figure out how to extricate yourself from this self-centered boor. You don't even know this person, so why would you care about all these details at this point? rude, awkward, ill mannered

Or sometimes someone I know will go into great long detail about someone I don't know, whom they recently ran into. Unless it's a fascinating story with a point, I zone out. Who cares? Give me a reason to care, and feed me any relevant details in interesting (I prefer fascinating) chunks, please.

In my editing, I'll sometimes see a new character come on scene, then the author stops the action to write paragraphs or even pages on the character, so we know where they grew up, their childhood situation, major in college, recent career moves, and love life. That's just so unnatural – and it brings the story to a skidding halt. And it's *telling*, not *showing*. There's nothing really going on in the present, as the story and action have been put on hold for this backstory dump.

Or some newbie authors start right out on the first page with background information ("telling") on the character, perhaps in the form of reminiscing, without anything interesting happening yet. Again, incite our curiosity about that person first by *showing* them

14

*interacting* with others in an intriguing scene with action, dialogue, and tension.

Another no-no is opening with your character on the way to somewhere or something eventful, but before he gets there, we get pages of info on his current or past life situation, as internal monologue or reminiscing. Just start the story! Then work in any interesting, relevant backstory info bit by bit as part of interaction or short thoughts or flashbacks.

We really don't need a lot of info right away on characters, even your protagonist and other important characters. Instead, introduce them in a natural, organic way, as you would meet new people in real life. You might form an immediate physical impression, especially if you find them attractive or repugnant. You notice whether they're tall or short, heavy or thin, well-groomed or scruffy. If you're interested in them, if you find them intriguing, you pay attention to them and maybe ask others about them. You gather info on them bit by bit, with lots of unanswered questions, which make you curious. Through conversation, you find out their opinions on things, and you formulate impressions of them based on what they say and how they're saying it, as well as their gestures, expressions, and actions.

Also, finding out about someone little by little raises questions and adds to the intrigue. What is that tidbit of info alluding to? What happened to her daughter? Unlike nonfiction, where readers read for information, in fiction readers want to be immersed in your story world, almost as if they are a part of that world. Get readers involved in trying to figure out the characters and their motivations and relationships. Don't dump a bunch of information on them. That's like giving a university lecture, not entertaining with engaging storytelling.

Think about a party or a meeting where you're standing back, observing what's going on while you wait for friends to arrive. You look around at who's there, listening in to snippets of conversation. A few people interest you, so you zoom in on them, trying not to be obvious. You might pick up on glances, smiles, frowns, rolling of eyes, and other facial expressions. You note their body language and that of others interacting with them.

Perhaps you decide to strike up a conversation with one or two. You find out about their personality and attitudes through their words, tone of voice, inflection, etc. Then, if they interest you, later you might ask about their job or personal situation and get filled in on a few details, colored of course by the attitudes and biases of the speaker. Maybe you hear a bit of gossip here and there, or they allude to someone else present and you pick up an undertone of envy or resentment or disdain.

Or think back to when you've just been hired at a company or joined a club or group, and you're attending your first meeting, trying to figure out who's who and what's expected of you. You observe the interactions and power struggles, perhaps pick up subtle resentments. Someone is complaining, someone else is on the defensive or nervous. You decide maybe those two are a couple (or want to be); the other two have some history as competitors or opponents; and so on.

That's how you should introduce your characters in your fiction, too. Not as the author intruding to present us with set impressions or paragraphs of backstory in a lump, but as the characters interacting with each other, with questions and answers, allusions to past issues and secrets. A character alone, thinking about what they've been through, isn't nearly as compelling, so keep those moments to small chunks at a time.

So curb those backstory dumps. Don't stop to give us the low-down on each character as he comes on the scene. Start with him interacting, and let snippets of info about him come out little by little, like in real life. Readers don't want to be told things, anyway. They want to be active participants, to draw their own conclusions based on how the characters are acting and interacting. And don't forget, the most interesting characters have secrets. Just hint at them; don't spill too much at any one time. Work in juicy tidbits and innuendos gradually, to keep readers on the edge of their seats.

Reveal your characters by their words and actions, with any significant physical traits thrown in, including any clothing that reveals character.

Give us a character in motion, then reveal her little by little, just like in real life.

① When describing a char, do you want to give the reader a cluster (block, chunk) of descriptive pts. Or is it better to weave in description as the story progresses? Called Onion skin method - Peeling layer by layer.

# Chapter 4 – Character Descriptions – Detailed or Sketchy?

## Are character descriptions barging in and interrupting your story?

Of course we need to know about the psychological makeup of your principal characters – their personality, motivations, hot-button triggers, strengths, weaknesses, fears, hopes, and goals. But what about detailed physical descriptions? There's a lot of debate about this, but it's definitely clunky to stop everything to describe a character in a paragraph or two. It's much more natural and sophisticated to work any relevant physical characteristics into the story line in a natural, organic way. Keep them as part of the ongoing action and interaction, not in a separate paragraph or cluster of descriptive sentences. And be sure to do it through the observations of the viewpoint character, colored by their personality and attitude, not as the author intruding to address the readers.

Some readers like the main characters of a story to be well-described, so they can visualize them. Others prefer only a few broad brush strokes so they can fill in the details themselves. But how much detail do we really need on minor characters, whose walk-on role may be confined to one scene or a few lines here and there throughout? Inserting detailed descriptions of each minor character as they appear on the scene, besides being unnecessary and appearing contrived, interrupts the action. It can also be confusing to the reader, who will then assume that, given the lengthy description, this character plays a more important role in the story and will likely reappear. So it's best not to confuse and subliminally annoy readers by describing minor characters in detail.

Even to suddenly interrupt the story to describe a main character in a paragraph or two seems unnatural and intrusive. To me, that's the author stepping in to address the readers, and it shatters our illusion of being right there in the story world with the characters. It's more sophisticated and organic to work in little details about the character as he or she is in action, interacting with others, rather than stopping everything for a static description. And be sure to include character reactions – theirs or someone else's. Is she self-conscious about her height? Does he wish he wasn't going bald?

### Describing noteworthy secondary characters

Here's an example of an introduction to a quirky, complex forensic pathologist who is discussing the cause of death of a young woman while performing an autopsy on an elderly homeless man.

We see the POV character, a doctor, interacting with the decidedly weird forensic pathologist he has to deal with regularly. Their conversation reveals a lot about both of them, including their opposing attitudes and contrasting personalities.

He set the heart down and held his hands wide, his shrill voice jubilant. "No froth, passive water distribution, and she checks out from hypoxia. It all fits." He slapped a gloved hand on the corpse's thigh. "Damn. This is effing awesome. When I nail this and write it up it will be the cover article in *Journal of Forensic Pathology*." He cackled and gave a fist pump.

"Damn it, Kip." Drake banged his fist on the metal instrument stand.

Kip flinched at the echoing crash.

"End the celebration. Now." Drake leaned forward. "We're talking about the death of my friend's wife."

Kip huffed and shot Drake a frown. "Jesus! Lighten up, man." He turned back to the corpse. "I told you before, I'm not into the feelings shit." He lifted a lung free of the chest cavity, the surface scarred and blackened. He held it aloft. "Check out this coal sack. The old drunk was a smoker. Color me surprised." He flopped the organ into the basin. "You don't find my emotional sensitivity acceptable, huh, ER? Well, excuse me all to hell. Who are ya, effing Oprah?"

Drake closed his eyes. Each medical specialty tended to attract certain types. Drake fought to save lives – Kip dealt with nothing but death. He hadn't talked to or treated a live patient in a decade. Perhaps his detachment was explainable.

"This is personal, Kip. Are you saying she was murdered?"

"I'm close, really close, to nailing this, feelings-guy." He shrugged. "What I do know for sure is that this death is so awesome it's giving me a hard-on."

Drake looked toward the ceiling. This wasn't a specialty thing – Kip was uniquely messed up.

This powerful intro to a unique character we want to hear more from is from Tom Combs' medical thriller, *Nerve Damage*.

How much or how little to describe main characters often boils down to personal preferences. For now, let's talk about how much to describe minor characters.

## Describing minor characters

Below are some examples, disguised, from a chapter in the middle of a novel to illustrate too much description of minor characters. All of the characters in this chapter appear in the book for the first and only time here. They're integral to this scene, but none of them reappears anywhere again in the book.

Here's the original scene from my editing of a thriller (names, locale, and circumstances changed).

The chapter opens:

Officer Lance Nakamoto of the LAPD scanned his rearview mirror for the other unmarked car behind him.

Nakamoto was a tallish Asian man in his mid-forties with short spiky black hair. He had a kind, friendly face that didn't

20

immediately give away his real profession. His height and athletic build suggested a retired football player or a bodyguard.

The four detectives pulled up in front of the suspect's house, got out, and approached the house.

Nakamoto rang the doorbell and then stepped back. His partner and second-in-command, Peter Carson, looked through the window of the house.

"The place has been trashed."

Carson was a hair shorter than Nakamoto, fair skinned, with plump red lips and expressive green eyes. His blond hair curled around his collar, and he wore fashionable horn-rimmed glasses. Although he was five years younger than Nakamoto, he was softer around the edges and not quite as fit as his boss.

Nakamoto took a look himself and saw ripped couches, overturned furniture, broken lamps and smashed pictures.

He turned to David Lewis, the third guy in the four-man team. "Climb that tree and see if you can get a look inside the second floor."

Lewis was in his early thirties, and at five feet seven inches, the shortest in the group. He had strawberry blond hair, tiny bird-like features and a lean frame that was more agile than powerful.

Lewis trotted over to the tall oak tree and started hoisting himself up. Nakamoto had all the necessary warrants to search the premises and apprehend Dovotnik if they found him, but for now they weren't sure how many were inside or whether they were dead or alive, so they were proceeding with caution.

In rewriting the above scene for this chapter, I drafted several versions, each with progressively less description.

First, I wrote this paragraph about their arrival:

Officer Lance Nakamoto of the LAPD pulled up in front of the suspect's house and turned off the ignition. He scanned his rearview mirror for the other unmarked car behind him, then checked his spiky black hair. As he waited for the other two to arrive, he turned to his partner, Carson, who had intense blue eyes and blond hair, in contrast to his own black eyes and hair. "Ready?"

Then I thought, if we're in Nakamoto's POV (which we are), is he really thinking about his partner's blue eyes and blond hair? Highly doubtful – they've just arrived at the scene of a crime. Ditto with checking his own hair. He's a cop at a stressful time, not a rock star.

Here's the same scene with a minimum of description of each character:

Officer Lance Nakamoto of the LAPD pulled up in front of the suspect's house and turned off the ignition. He scanned his rearview mirror for the other unmarked car behind him, then turned to his partner, Carson. "Ready?"

Carson patted his gun. "You bet."

The other car pulled up and the four detectives got out and approached the house.

Nakamoto rang the doorbell and then stepped back. They waited. Nothing. Carson looked through the window of the house. "The place has been trashed."

Nakamoto took a look himself and saw ripped couches, overturned furniture, broken lamps and smashed pictures.

He turned to David Lewis, the third guy in the four-man team. "Lewis, you're young and agile. Climb that tree and see if you can get a look inside the second floor."

Lewis trotted over to the tall oak tree and started hoisting himself up.

Nakamoto had warrants to search the premises and apprehend Dovotnik if they found him, but for now they weren't sure how many were inside or whether they were dead or alive, so they were proceeding with caution.

Of course, this scene and the description could be written in a number of effective ways. You could probably pare it down some

22

more. The main point is that for minor characters, it's usually best to include only the most obvious or relevant traits, and as an aside, a natural part of the ongoing action.

**Don't give minor characters too much airtime or describe them in too much detail, or readers will think they play a more significant role.**

Here's another well-disguised example from my editing, where a neighbor, who only appears again briefly, was given too much attention.

> Jack grabbed his coat and headed out to his car, parked in the driveway.
>
> His neighbor Harold was in his front yard next door, with his customary baseball cap glued to his head, wearing a yellow golf shirt and green plaid pants.
>
> Some thought Harold a little eccentric. He was a golf fanatic and an avid fisherman. He could talk your ear off about any sport, in fact.
>
> "Mornin', Jack."

Besides giving a minor character significance disproportionate to his role in the novel, the above description also slows down the forward momentum of the story. Jack was headed out in a hurry, so it doesn't make sense for him to be spending so much time thinking about his neighbor. And the interruption shifts the readers' attention from Jack's urgent goal to his neighbor, making us wonder how that guy figures into the plot.

If you gave a minor char. significance that is disproportionate to his/her role, what would you also be doing? (A) Slowing down the forward momentum of the story.

# Chapter 5 – Character Descriptions: Learn from the Pros

## TIPS FOR CHARACTER DEPICTIONS THAT INTRIGUE

As mentioned in the previous chapter, in my editing of fiction, I find my clients often tend to over-describe characters, with too much emphasis on specific visual details. Readers like to be active participants in the reading experience. They enjoy the challenge and satisfaction of piecing things together and drawing their own conclusions about characters.

### Show, don't tell.

Rather than giving readers a lengthy, detailed police line-up description of a character's height, build, facial features, and clothing, it's best to just show the "essence" of the character, including his personality or state of mind, as perceived by the viewer, through a few well-chosen details. Then let the readers imagine the rest themselves.

For example, in James Scott Bell's novelette, *Force of Habit*, sassy, rebellious nun Sister J arrives at a house looking for an unhappy little girl who was kicked out of her school. A man answers the door. Bell shows us Sister J's immediate impression with a few apt, well-chosen words:

> A man of thirty or thirty-five, swarthy, a face like a belt sander, answered.

A "face like a belt sander" says it all, doesn't it.

Then, a few paragraphs down, we see how belligerent he is to Sister J's efforts to help his young niece:

He set his jaw like a fist ready to jab.

And here's how Nora Roberts describes the appearance of a stranger, in *Hot Rocks*:

> A heroic belch of thunder followed the strange little man into the shop. He glanced around apologetically, as if the rude noise were his responsibility rather than nature's, and fumbled a package under his arm so he could close a black-and-white-striped umbrella.
>
> Both umbrella and man dripped, somewhat mournfully, onto the neat square of mat just inside the door. ... He stood where he was, as if not entirely sure of his welcome.

We readers might all visualize this man a bit differently, to suit our own ideas of what he should look like, but we get an immediate impression of his timidity and hesitancy, which is all we really need at this point.

And here's a depiction of a prematurely aging middle-aged woman that strikes to the core, with a few masterful brush strokes. In *Moonlight Mile*, instead of saying, "She looked old for her age, with her white hair and wrinkles," Dennis Lehane describes her like this:

> I did some quick math and guessed she was about fifty. These days, fifty might be the new forty, but in her case it was the new sixty. Her once-strawberry hair was white. The lines in her face were deep enough to hide gravel in. She had the air of someone clinging to a wall of soap.

**Show the viewpoint character's feelings and reactions to the character he/she is observing.**

Also, work in the viewer's emotional reaction to the character. Is the narrator impressed? Intimidated? Fearful? Attracted to them? Disgusted or repulsed?

For example, Brad Parks, in *The Girl Next Door*, describes the first-person narrator's feelings about a love interest:

> ...in addition to being fun, smart, and quick-witted – in a feisty way that always kept me honest – she's quite easy to look at, with never-ending legs, toned arms, curly brown hair, and eyes that tease and smile and glint all at the same time.

By contrast, the protagonist of Dennis Lehane's *Moonlight Mile* describes a spoiled rich kid who leaves victims in his wake without a second thought, as Mummy and Daddy will clean up after him. Here, the disgust of the observer character comes through loud and clear:

> Brandon wasn't your run-of-the-mill rich kid asshole. He worked double shifts at it.

The investigator paid to spy on him goes on to describe the kid's clothes:

> Brandon wore a manufacturer-stained, manufacturer-faded hoodie that retailed for around $900 over a white silk T with a collar dragged down by a pair of $600 shades. His baggy shorts also had little rips in them, compliments of whichever nine-year-old Indonesian had been poorly paid to put them there.

Lehane's astute investigator later describes a trophy-wife stepmother:

> She had the look of a woman who kept her plastic surgeon on speed dial. Her breasts were prominently displayed in most of the photos and looked like perfect softballs made of flesh. Her forehead was unlined in the way of the recently embalmed and her smile resembled that of someone undergoing electroshock.

**Appeal to the senses.**

Also, to bring the character and scene alive for the readers, evoke as many of the senses as are appropriate for the situation, not just visual impressions. Is their perfume cloying, or their body odor overpowering? Is their voice high-pitched or raspy? Their hand cold and clammy?

James Lee Burke's protagonist, Detective Dave Robicheaux, meets a penitentiary guard in his novel, *The Neon Rain*. Notice how Burke mixes it up and appeals to several senses.

> His khaki sleeves were rolled over his sunburned arms, and he had the flat green eyes and heavy facial features of north Louisiana hill people. He smelled faintly of dried sweat, Red Man, and talcum powder.

And here's a great example from Sandra Brown, in *Smoke Screen*:

> Raley stepped into the one-room cabin. It smelled of fried pork and the mouse-gnawed Army blanket on the cot in the corner.
>
> It took a moment for his eyes to adjust to the dimness and find the old man. He was sitting at a three-legged table, hunched over a cup of coffee like a dog guarding a hard-won bone, staring into the snowy screen of a black-and-white television. Ghostly images flickered in and out. There was no audio except for a static hiss.

I feel like I'm right there in that dark, tiny cabin with the old man. Don't you?

**Give an overall emotional impression, rather than a lot of specific factual details.**

When we first see or meet someone, we don't take a detailed mental inventory from top to toe of their height, build, hair style and color, eyes, facial features, and what they're wearing. Usually one or two features stand out and grab our attention, along with obvious

27

aspects of their personality and our immediate emotional reaction to them.

Dennis Lehane gives an immediate impression of two sharply contrasting people in a few choice words in his novel, *A Drink Before the War*:

The narrator (POV character) has walked into a bar and is being introduced to two senators.

> Sterling Mulkern was a florid, beefy man, the kind who carried weight like a weapon, not a liability. He had a shock of stiff white hair you could land a DC-10 on and a handshake that stopped just short of inducing paralysis. ...
> Brian Paulson was rake thin, with smooth hair the color of tin and a wet fleshy handshake.... His greeting was a nod and a blink, befitting someone who'd stepped out of the shadows only momentarily.

In the hands of a master like Lehane, we get an immediate, powerful impression of each of these men through a handful of perfectly chosen, evocative words.

**Reveal the character's personality, goals, and intentions by their actions and words, rather than telling the readers what they're like.**

Let's go back to James Lee Burke and *The Neon Rain*.

Detective Dave Robicheaux is at a penitentiary to visit a man on death row. A guard opens the cell door for Dave, who studies the condemned man.

> His wiry gray and black hair was dripping with sweat, and his face was the color and texture of old paper. He looked up at me from where he was seated on his bunk, and his eyes were hot and bright and moisture was beaded across his upper lip. He held a Camel cigarette between his yellowed fingers, and the floor around his feet was covered with cigarette butts.

Instead of telling us the prisoner was nervous, Burke shows this subtly and masterfully with well-chosen sensory and visual details.

Burke continues a few lines down:

> His hands clutched his thighs and he looked at the floor, then back at me. I saw him swallow.
> "How scared you ever been?" he said.

Burke paints such a powerful picture with an economy of words that we feel this man's terror at facing the electric chair, without Burke telling us "he was scared" or "he was terrified."

So, when introducing new characters, remember to show their essence mainly through their actions, words, and attitude, and a few well-chosen, evocative descriptors, rather than telling too much.

Also, be sure to filter your character descriptions through the mood, attitude, and reactions of the viewer, the POV character for the scene. This serves to add to the characterization of the viewpoint character.

1) What are the 5 main techniques for telling the short story?

2) What is a back story?

3)

# PART II

# HOOK READERS WITH A RIVETING OPENING

# Chapter 6 – To Prologue or Not to Prologue?

Should you include a prologue at the beginning of your novel, before Chapter one? Consider carefully before doing so.

For most genres, prologues seem to have fallen out of favor. Agents generally don't like them, and many readers tend to skip them, mainly because in the past they've often been tedious. Today, prologues seem to be more accepted in fantasy, speculative fiction, and historical fiction, where a lot of world-building is needed, but be sure to keep them short and intriguing. For most other genres, it's probably best to skip the prologue and start right in with Chapter one. Or, if your prologue is both necessary and compelling, consider renaming it chapter one, or just present it before Chapter one, without naming it "Prologue."

Here's what some literary agents have to say on the subject of prologues:

> "I'm not a fan of prologues, preferring to find myself in the midst of a moving plot on page one rather than being kept outside of it, or eased into it."
>
> ~ Michelle Andelman, Regal Literary

> "Most agents hate prologues. Just make the first chapter relevant and well written."
>
> ~ Andrea Brown, Andrea Brown Literary Agency

> "Prologues are usually a lazy way to give backstory chunks to the reader and can be handled with more finesse throughout the story. Damn the prologue, full speed ahead!"
>
> ~ Laurie McLean, Foreword Literary

"At least 50% of prologues that I see in sample material don't work and aren't necessary. Make sure there's a real reason to use one."
~ Jenny Bent, literary agent

And finally, Nathan Bransford, publishing guru, tells it like he sees it:

"A prologue is three to five pages of introductory material that is written while the author is procrastinating from writing a more difficult section of the book."

What exactly is a prologue, anyway? Merriam-Webster defines it as "the preface or introduction to a literary work." I don't know about you, but I rarely read prefaces or introductions, whether to fiction or nonfiction. I prefer to jump right into the actual story (or in the case of nonfiction, I go straight to the Table of Contents).

Prologues can be as short as a line or two or as long as several pages, although the latter is not recommended. They often serve to set up the story or provide background info or scenes on events that occurred earlier, even much earlier, and possibly even in a different locale. Prologues can be told in a different voice from the rest of the story, about different characters, possibly ancestors of the story characters. Or they might feature the story characters when they were much younger.

Of course, you can accomplish all these things without a prologue. For example, you can use flashbacks within the story to show scenes from the past, or convey information about the past through dialogue or character thoughts. Or perhaps a character discovers a diary or an old newspaper and reads excerpts from it.

Why do agents and editors generally discourage prologues?

One big reason is that traditionally, prologues have often taken the form of long, boring, information dumps, the author's way of quickly (for him) establishing a story world and providing background info. But fiction readers don't like to be told things.

They much prefer to be entertained and swept immediately into a story world through compelling scenes, with lots of conflict and tension. They may feel mildly irritated that they're expected to read something else, especially if it's almost all description or explaining, before they can jump into the actual story. Some readers may even decide to skip the whole book if it starts with a lengthy prologue without action or dialogue, basically the author addressing the readers, which is not engrossing fiction.

Also, most readers don't want a barrier or delay between them and the "real" story. They want to jump right into the heart of the main narrative.

So if you really want to include a prologue, make sure it's not a lengthy, "telling" information dump of background on the characters or the situation. That's a sign of lazy writing, and not a good introduction to your storytelling skills, your voice, or your tale. If you choose to use a prologue, make sure it's necessary (information the readers need to know before the story begins), short (I'd keep it to less than two pages), and a riveting scene, with fascinating characters and action and dialogue. Take the same care to hook the readers that you would with the first pages of Chapter one. Remember that your primary job is to draw readers into the tale right after they pick up the book – or they might put it down and pick up another.

If your existing prologue is a lot of explaining backstory, either rewrite it as a compelling scene or delete it there and introduce that info little by little in the course of your first twelve chapters or so.

If readers can visually see that the prologue is short and has lots of white space, indicating dialogue and action, they're much more likely to read it. Also, don't write your prologue in italics, as lengthy passages in italics can be tiring for the eyes and could subliminally irritate some readers.

The most important thing is to find out how readers of your genre feel about prologues and whether they skip them. Do they feel they add to the quality and enjoyment of the read or are they an impediment before the story? It would be a good thing to ask your beta readers that specific question – would they like your story better with or without the prologue? And could most of that info be imparted within the story in a more dynamic, compelling, organic way?

So, to decide whether to include a prologue at the beginning of your novel, consider the norms and expectations of the genre, and also the fact that prologues are generally in disfavor these days. Ask yourself whether the preamble is necessary or the information can be more effectively introduced within the story itself, through brief flashbacks, character thoughts, dialogue, or short excerpts from diaries, newspapers,and other texts.

If you feel it's necessary, make sure it accomplishes your purpose in a relatively short, compelling scene, with action and dialogue. Make sure it draws the readers in, rather than pushing them away.

Note: Just as this book was going to press, I discovered an excellent blog post on prologues by Janice Hardy of Fiction University, called "Pondering the Prologue: Keep it or Kill it?" Do check it out.

① Show a campus diva walking across the set on "Set Friday." "If we don't need to go see her for ourselves, you are successful.
② Show your best friend @ dinner

5 Narrative modes – DATED
5 Senses : ① Sight, ② Taste, ③ Touch, ④ Sound, ⑤ Smell

# Chapter 7 – Open Your Novel in Your Protagonist's Head

In past centuries, the more leisurely, distanced storytelling tradition was to first describe the setting, followed by a kind of authorial overview of the situation and characters, and finally show us the main character and his current situation. Today's best-selling authors, for the most part, have gotten away from that type of cinematic opening.

As literary agent and writing guru Donald Maass says in *The Fire in Fiction*, about rejecting submissions: "Too many manuscripts begin at a distance from their protagonists, as if opening with a long shot like in a movie. That's a shame. Why keep readers at arm's length?"

He continues, "Novels are unique among art forms in their intimacy. They can take us inside a character's heart and mind right away. And that is where your readers want to be. Go there immediately."

Unlike readers of past decades, who weren't bombarded all day with every kind of distracting media competing for their attention, today's readers are less patient with rambling beginnings. They want to open a book and get immediately drawn into the character's problems.

So nowadays, it's more immediate and compelling to start right out in your protagonist's head and show him or her in motion, with attitude, actions, reactions and feelings. That way your reader, rather than being held at a distance while you introduce the setting, starts to become emotionally engaged right away, and gets hooked in quickly, absorbed in your story, wanting to find out more.

Your first paragraph should be dynamic, not a meandering lead-up to something more interesting. Don't rev your engines by starting your story with your character waking up to an ordinary day, or on the way to somewhere, with no tension. It's more intriguing to readers if you open with the protagonist challenged somehow and the plot already moving forward. Also, an interaction with someone else, with some tension involved, is more compelling than internal musings, reflections, or thoughts about the weather or even upcoming events.

And it's best to get into the point of view of your protagonist right away, not some other character's, and stay there for the first chapter. Readers start to identify with and bond with the first character they read about and start worrying about them. If that person then gets killed off at the end of the chapter, or turns out to be a minor or even supporting character, many readers will feel cheated.

By starting with your main character's name, in their head, you quickly answer the reader's first question, "Whose story is this?" Don't keep them wondering, trying to figure it out – that can be frustrating. They want to know who to root for right off the bat, so they can relax and start enjoying the story.

Similarly, start each new chapter or scene with the name of the POV character for that scene, so we know right away who we're concentrating on in this scene, whose head we're in.

Also, I advise against starting with "the detective" or "the police officer" or "the private investigator" or "the movie star" or some other anonymous, third-party, distancing description of your lead character, without their name attached. That immediately creates an emotional distance from the character that can throw the reader off. Sure, use their title or other descriptor, but start right out in your protagonist's head, and use his name. As Jack M. Bickham says in *The 38 Most Common Fiction Writing Mistakes*, "Figure out whose story it is. Get inside that character right away – and stay there [for most of the story]."

Here are some examples of first lines / paragraphs of best-selling novels that start right out in the point of view of the protagonist of the novel.

Lee Child, *The Hard Way*:

"Jack Reacher ordered espresso, double, no peel, no cube, foam cup, no china, and before it arrived at his table he saw a man's life change forever."

Louise Penny, *Bury Your Dead*:

"Up the stairs they raced, taking them two at a time, trying to be as quiet as possible. Gamache struggled to keep his breathing steady, …"

David Baldacci, *Hell's Corner*:

"Oliver Stone was counting seconds, an exercise that had always calmed him. And he needed to be calm."

Lisa Gardner, *Love You More*:

"Sergeant Detective D.D. Warren prided herself on her excellent investigative skills."

Andrew Gross, *The Dark Tide*:

"As the morning sun canted sharply through the bedroom window, Charles Friedman dropped the baton. He hadn't had the dream in years, yet there he was, gangly, twelve years old, running…"

Katherine Neville, *The Fire*:

"Solarin gripped his little daughter's mittened hand firmly in his own. He could hear the snow crunch beneath his boots and see their breath rise in silvery puffs, as together they crossed…"

Steve Berry, *The Paris Vendetta*:

"The bullet tore into Cotton Malone's left shoulder. He fought to ignore the pain and focused on the plaza. People rushed in all directions. Horns blared. Tires squealed."

Karin Slaughter, *Fallen*:

"Faith Mitchell dumped the contents of her purse onto the passenger seat of her Mini, trying to find something to eat. [..] The computer seminar she'd attended this morning was supposed to last only three hours, but..."

Lee Child, *Tripwire*:

"Jack Reacher saw the guy step in through the door."

Robert Beatty, *Serafina and the Black Cloak*:

"Serafina opened her eyes and scanned the darkened workshop, looking for any rats stupid enough to come into her territory while she slept..."

Of course, we can all think of excellent novels that take several paragraphs or even pages to establish the POV character, but in general, delaying this vital info is on the decline. Aspiring authors who intend to go the agent and publisher route especially need to consider the short attention span of busy, time-pressured professionals, most of whom won't read past the first page if it confuses or bores them.

# Chapter 8 – Your First Pages Are Critical

Once you've finished the first draft of your novel or short story, it's time to go back to the very beginning. Your first five pages are absolutely critical. Most agents and acquiring editors, like readers, will stop reading by the fifth page – if not sooner – if the story and characters don't captivate them.

Agents get tens of thousands of submissions a year, and if you don't grab them within the first page or two, the sad reality is that your book will probably be rejected. As readers, most of us will read the back cover and maybe the first page, then decide based on that whether to buy the book or not. And even when I've paid money for a book, if it doesn't grab me by about page ten or fifteen, I'll discard it.

I receive several first chapters of novels every week – often two or three per day – as submissions for possible editing, and I always read the first page. Some are clear and compelling and make me want to read more. But too often, one of two main problems emerges within the first few pages. Either the author spends too much time revving his engine with description or backstory before we even care (boring), or the opposite – we're plunged right into the heart of the action but have no idea where we are or what's going on (confusing).

Also, I've judged short stories for Writer's Digest's Popular Fiction contest and other contests and anthologies, and I know from experience that if the first page isn't intriguing and polished, there's little point in reading more. In the latest WD contest, I could only choose ten best stories out of 147 submitted, and I had less than a month to do it, so if the first page was boring, confusing, or full of errors, that story went to the "reject" pile. Only those that stood out as top-quality storytelling combined with skillful, error-free writing went to the "maybe" or "for sure" pile.

There are three cardinal rules of successful novelists:

- Don't bore your reader.
- Don't confuse your reader.
- Don't annoy your reader.

I've discussed the detrimental effects of starting off too slow, with too much description or backstory, elsewhere. In this chapter, I'll focus on the other problem that can turn readers off – fuzzy beginnings.

One of the main reasons agents, acquiring editors and readers will reject a book after reading the first few pages is that they're confused. They need to be able to visualize right away whose story it is, what's going on, and roughly where and when the story is taking place. It's frustrating not being able to form a mental picture quickly of the person, their role in the story, the locale, and the general situation.

**Set up your story in the first paragraphs.**

Not only does your first page need to hook your reader in, set the tone for the rest of the book, and demonstrate your writing ability and style, but the reader needs to know right away whose story it is and where and when it's taking place. That way, they can get situated, then relax and start enjoying the story. If they have a lot of questions, they're going to start getting frustrated and may put down your book by the end of the first page or two. Readers want to be able to get into a good story right away, not have to spend the first several pages – or more – trying to figure out what's going on.

Try to work in the basics of the **5 W's** on your first page – **who, what, where, when,** and **why**, preferably within the first two or three paragraphs. Give the readers a quick snapshot, without going into a great deal of detail yet. Provide them just enough info to get oriented so they're not totally confused and can start enjoying the story. The trick is to create a definite scene while leaving out enough info to pique readers' curiosity and raise questions that keep them turning the pages.

**Here are the 5 W's in action:**

### ~ Who? Whose story is it?

It's almost always best to open the novel in the viewpoint of your primary character. Why? Because the first person the readers read about is the person they start identifying with. They'll feel cheated if after they've invested time getting to know this person and bonding a bit with him, he suddenly turns out to be not someone they should be rooting for at all. Perhaps he's the antagonist, whom they're supposed to be hating, or a minor character – or, even worse, someone who gets killed off a little while later.

As Steve Berry, best-selling author and sought-after writing workshop leader, tells participants, "Always start your book in the point of view of your protagonist." I think this is excellent advice, as the readers – not to mention agents and acquiring editors – want to know right away whose story it is, who to start bonding with and cheering for.

**~ What?** What's going on? What is he doing, exactly? Can the reader visualize the situation? If not, add a few details.

Without drowning us in long, descriptive passages right at the beginning, give the readers a few hints early on – definitely on the first page – of the setting of your story. Don't confuse and frustrate your readers by making them wonder where on earth all this is happening, and whether it's in the present or some other time.

**~ Where?** Where is he? What's the overall setting – which continent, country, state/province, city/town? Is it an urban or rural setting? Or in the wilderness, at sea, on a desert, in the jungle, on a mountaintop? And if inside a building, is it an office building? A log cabin? At home? What kind of house? Which room? It can be annoying for a reader to start a story with lengthy dialogue and have no idea where the speakers are.

~ **When?** Is this story taking place in the present? The future? The past? How far in the past? What season? What month? In the morning? Afternoon? Evening? Middle of the night?

## Why? Why should I care about this character?

Readers aren't going to invest time and emotional energy reading a story about a character they don't like or can't identify with. Be sure your protagonist is at least somewhat likeable and sympathetic, so readers will care about her. And make her well-rounded and multi-layered, with hopes and fears, strengths and weaknesses, secrets and inner conflict. And have her confronted with a problem or challenge – an inciting incident – within the first few pages, as conflict is what drives fiction forward. A perfect character with an ideal life is both annoying and boring – not a formula for compelling fiction.

## Why should I read this story?

You need to entice readers with your style, tone, and content in your first five pages or so. Draw the reader in with a great first scene, well-written, with interesting, complex characters, some intriguing action, and compelling, natural-sounding dialogue. Include an inciting incident and initial conflict, and hint at greater problems to come. Introduce or hint at a worthy adversary – a cunning villain or attractive but maddening / annoying possible love interest. And be sure to write your first pages in the same tone, style, and voice (suspenseful, humorous, serious, romantic, etc.) you'll use for the rest of the novel, so the readers will have a good idea of whether they're going to enjoy this book.

**And be sure to set the tone for the whole story.** Your first page is also a kind of promise to your readers. They want to get a feel quickly for your writing style and your handling of the genre to know whether they'll like it or not. Be sure that your first page reflects the overall tone, style, and voice of the novel, and even hints at aspects like the level of violence, profanities, and sex scenes they can expect. Then keep your promise by delivering for the rest of the novel. If your novel starts out as a romance, then veers into horror, you're going to have some pretty upset and even disgusted readers. Same thing if your action-adventure turns into a schmaltzy love story.

But don't get bogged down trying to perfect your opening pages in the early stages – wait until you've got all or most of your first draft written. By then, you'll be "in the groove" and you'll know your character and her problems a lot better, as well as the resolution, so this part will flow so much more easily.

To conclude, here's some excellent advice from best-selling novelist and writing instructor Steven James:

**Evaluate your hook:**

With each story you start, always remember that an effective story opening needs to do seven things:

- Grab the readers' attention.
- Introduce a character readers will care about.
- Set the story's mood.
- Establish the storyteller's voice.
- Orient readers to the world of the protagonist (and enable them to picture it).
- Lock in the genre.
- End in a way that is both surprising and satisfying.

– These 7 points are from "5 Story Mistakes Even Good Writers Make" by Steven James, Writer's Digest magazine (March 2012)

① In terms of p.o.v. what's the advice 4 beg. writers?

A. One P.O.V. per scene.

② Why is the omniscient P.O.V. not as popular?

A. Author gets into too many heads & tells too much.

③ What is author's intrusion?

A. When author tells too much

# PART III

# USE DEEP POINT OF VIEW TO ENGAGE READERS

④ Which is the most effective p.o.v. to write in?

A. 3rd per - past tense.

⑤ State 3 disadvantages of writing in 1st per.

① What is p.o.v.?

Narrator's perception of events in the story

# Chapter 9 – Introduction to Point of View in Fiction

## What is point of view?

Basically, in fiction, point of view or viewpoint (also called POV) simply refers to who's narrating the story, or from whose viewpoint the scene is being told; in other words, through whose unique perspective and attitudes the story events are viewed, related and slanted.

In today's terms, it's about whose head and body we the readers are in for any given scene or chapter, reacting along with the character as events unfold.

Sol Stein provides this definition in *How to Grow a Novel*: "Point of view, or POV, is simply the perspective from which a scene is written, which character's eyes and mind are witnessing the event."

Point of view is almost always slanted – events are recounted from a personal viewpoint, colored by the POV character's emotions and attitudes. Think of the daily interactions of a mismatched couple leading up to a nasty divorce, with violent arguments and fights. How would the events leading up to it be related by the wife as opposed to the husband? How about through the eyes of a third person, like a child huddled in his bedroom? Or the wife's sister or the husband's brother? Or a neighbor? What about through a more detached account of events, such as would be written by a mediator or lawyer? Each recounting would be a different story, with different details stressed and others downplayed or conveniently left out.

If the wife or husband decided to write their side of the story in a journal or as a memoir, they'd use first person or "I" and "me." But if they decided to write a short story or novel based on those years, they might narrate it in third person. The wife's viewpoint would be narrated using "she," for example. This is called "third-person limited" point of view. As this character-narrator is deeply invested in the story, both of these techniques would likely be close third-person point of view or deep POV, with the character's feelings and inner reactions shown throughout.

If for some reason they commissioned a neighbor or the mediator or lawyer to write an account of it, this would be omniscient point of view – the story would be told by someone all-knowing outside the characters. The writer/narrator could also interview characters for their words and thoughts at the time, then include dialogue and character inner reactions. Omniscient point of view is like the author talking to the readers, explaining things to us, rather than the characters telling their own story.

In contemporary fiction, point of view (or POV) simply refers to the character through whose perspective the story events are related. Ideally, we should only see, hear, smell, feel, and experience events as that character would – with no additional information provided "from above" by the author. This closeness helps readers get to know the viewpoint character intimately, which makes them start worrying about him – and that keeps them turning the pages.

Here's a basic rundown of various viewpoint possibilities:

## OMNISCIENT POINT OF VIEW

In the nineteenth and early twentieth centuries, novels were usually told from a distant authorial point of view, hovering over everything. In omniscient (all-knowing) point of view, the author is looking down at events from a god-like perspective, relating the story directly to the readers, often from outside the perspective of any of the characters.

Using cinematic techniques, the story may open by viewing a whole valley or city as if from way above, then slowly move in closer to

46

perhaps show a particular neighborhood, then a family, then the individual family members. We can suddenly be in one character's thoughts and, in the same scene, another character's, and perhaps more. But the narrator doesn't spend a lot of time with any one character, so this tends to be a distant perspective, and readers are rarely able to get to know one character intimately.

The omniscient narrator knows everything about the characters and can enter the minds of any of them, whenever he chooses. He knows everything that has happened, is happening, and will happen, and has complete freedom to move through time in any direction.

Some classic novels written mostly in omniscient viewpoint include *War and Peace, Little Women, Pride and Prejudice, Gone With the Wind, Tom Jones, Vanity Fair, A Tale of Two Cities, Oliver Twist, Bleak House,* and *Anna Karenina.*

**Example of omniscient POV: *Little Women,* by Louisa May Alcott:**

The narrator of *Little Women* (published in 1869) is an omniscient voice that tells the readers about the setting and the various characters, including their thoughts and feelings, as if from an all-seeing, all-knowing viewpoint. It's the author, Louisa May Alcott, telling us a story as if we were sitting around the campfire listening to her.

In the first chapter, the author-narrator describes the setting, then each of the March sisters, in order from oldest to youngest, as the girls sit by the fire knitting. Notice how the narrator-author addresses the readers directly, and refers to herself as "we" in this omniscient storytelling voice:

> As young readers like to know 'how people look', we will take this moment to give...a little sketch of the four sisters, who sat knitting away in the twilight, while the December snow fell quietly without, and the fire crackled cheerfully within. It was a comfortable room, though the carpet was faded and the furniture very plain...

Margaret, the eldest of the four, was sixteen, and very pretty, being plump and fair, with large eyes, plenty of soft brown hair, a sweet mouth, and white hands, of which she was rather vain. Fifteen-year-old Jo was very tall, thin, and brown, and reminded one of a colt, for she never seemed to know what to do with her long limbs, which were very much in her way. [. . .] Elizabeth, or Beth, as everyone called her, was a rosy, smooth-haired, bright-eyed girl of thirteen, with a shy manner, a timid voice, and a peaceful expression which was seldom disturbed. [. . .] Amy, though the youngest, was a most important person, in her own opinion at least.

When I was ten or twelve years old, I loved this story. But if I were to read it for the first time today, I'd find it jarring and unnatural-sounding, and would wonder why the author is butting into the story so much to tell us things. And why are we jumping around from one person's thoughts to another's within a scene? To me, that's irritating and confusing. Most of today's readers would prefer to delve deeper into the viewpoint of one primary character, or maybe two. So if the above scene were recounted today, it would likely be shown from the perspective of Jo March, as she looks around at her sisters and her mother and feels the chilly draft coming in under the door and around the windows and moves in closer to enjoy the warmth from the fireplace. Then other chapters might be told from the POV of other important characters, like her mother, one of her sisters, or Laurie, their young male friend.

A somewhat similar and more believable effect can be achieved today through a more conventional third-person multiple viewpoint technique – different chapters being shown from the point of view of different characters, with varying degrees of closeness. The chapters dedicated to the main character would be in a tighter, more intimate viewpoint than those from the perspective of the antagonist, for example.

Omniscient point of view is no longer in favor in most of today's popular fiction (a main exception being historical sagas, which have

48

a broader scope), as this technique is too distancing for today's readers, who prefer to identify with the most important character of the story. And jumping from one viewpoint to another within a scene ("head-hopping") can be confusing to readers, and prevents us from bonding with one main character.

A handful of best-selling authors today have the skills to allow the point of view to flow back and forth between characters within a scene, but in most cases, especially for new writers, it's best to stick to one point of view per scene.

For today's readership, who are used to a more anchored, intimate point of view, omniscient POV can seem implausible and unrealistic, almost cheating. Nowadays, readers generally prefer close (or deep) POV so we can connect strongly with the lead character of the novel. Deep point of view also mimics how each of us sees the world around us, from our own limited visual and auditory viewpoint, filtering everything through our particular worldview, attitudes, personality, and mood.

Aspiring fiction writers today sometimes write in a shaky kind of omniscient POV because they still haven't honed their fiction writing skills to the point of knowing how to use viewpoint effectively.

Editor and author Sol Stein calls omniscient point of view "the undisciplined free verse of beginners... Because the writer flits about from character to character, often thoughtlessly, the result can be more like alphabet soup than a controlled experience for the reader. Most inexpert fiction that has come my way is maimed by uncontrolled third-person or omniscient point of view." (*How to Grow a Novel*)

## FIRST-PERSON POINT OF VIEW

First-person POV is where the narrator is the main character, and he's telling us his story using "I," "me," and "we" – "I pushed through the crowds on the busy street. Someone tapped me on the shoulder, so I turned around." Since the character is talking directly to the readers, this is the most intimate, immediately involving mode. Memoirs and some novels are written in first-person, past tense, and first-person present tense is popular in young adult (YA) fiction these days: "As I hurry down the street, I hear a car honking, and someone is calling out my name."

First-person narration is challenging to do well, as you need a character who is strong enough and unique enough to carry a whole novel without readers getting tired of listening to him or her. And if they're really weird and quirky, readers may find their voice a bit irritating after several chapters. Also, you as the writer have to "become" this character, without having them be a clone of you. It's difficult to get right inside the head and body of a character who is very different from you, but if he's very similar to you, you risk boring or disenchanting readers who may well pick up on this and think you're narcissistic.

## SECOND-PERSON POINT OF VIEW

Second-person POV is where the protagonist, instead of saying "I," is saying "you" – "You walk in the room and all eyes are upon you. You glance around looking for Jayne, but she's not there." This viewpoint is generally considered literary and "artsy," and is rarely used in fiction, and for good reason: it's talking to the reader as if the reader is a character in the story. So it comes across as an artificial literary device used to show cleverness of approach and originality of thought. The problem with that is it makes the reader aware of the author's writing techniques rather than getting lost in the story, which is the whole objective of compelling fiction. It might also make you feel like you're reading an instructional article – first you do this, then you do that. That said, I recently read a short story by best-selling author Steven James that was so gripping I soon forgot it was written in second-person.

## THIRD-PERSON POINT OF VIEW

Third-person POV is by far the most common viewpoint in contemporary fiction, and is usually combined with past tense: "He

50

walked up the steps and rang the doorbell. She opened the door and looked at him in surprise."

Third-person is easier than first person to do effectively, as you can include various characters' viewpoints. But of course, be sure to give the primary character more airtime, and give other POV characters each his or her own scene (multiple viewpoints). Also, stick to one point of view per scene.

Close third-person point of view draws the readers in tighter and creates more intimacy with the character. This is also called deep point of view, and I get into it in greater detail in the following chapters.

Third person, past tense, with close point of view, is the most common storytelling choice in current popular fiction. Usually, we're in the head of the main character for most of the story, and only see, hear, and feel what he does. We can also be in the POV of other important characters, like the love interest or a close friend or family member, or the antagonist. But be sure to feature them "from the inside" in their own scenes or chapters, not all mixed together in one scene. This is called multiple POV. Some authors opt to use first-person ("I") for the protagonist and then switch to third person (he or she) for chapters told through another character's POV.

**Using both third and first-person within one novel:** *Mixed P.O.V.*

Some writers use various different first-person viewpoints in a story, changing to another character's point of view in a new chapter. This is difficult to pull off well, since they're all "I," so they need to have radically different personalities and voices. Some novelists will mainly use first-person for the protagonist and then throw in some third-person scenes or chapters in the POV of other characters. Either way, I find this technique more distracting than when all viewpoints are in third person.

51

# Chapter 10 – The Pros and Cons of First-Person Point of View

As mentioned in the previous chapter, most novels are written in third-person past tense: "He raced through the dark alley, the footsteps getting louder behind him." First-person is another option: "As I slammed down the phone in disgust, I heard the doorbell ring."

While first-person viewpoint can be ideal for a short story, writing a novel-length story in first-person is riskier, especially for a beginner. New fiction writers sometimes opt to write their novel in first-person, as they think this will be easier. But writing a novel effectively and compellingly in first-person is a lot more difficult than it appears, for a number of reasons. As best-selling novelist David Morrell points out in *The Successful Novelist*, "If the first person were as easy as it seems, all stories would be written from that viewpoint."

Some examples of well-known novels written in first-person point of view include,

in the 19th Century:

*Moby-Dick* by Herman Melville (1851), *Great Expectations* by Charles Dickens (1860), *Notes from Underground* by Fyodor Dostoevsky (1864), and *Adventures of Huckleberry Finn* by Mark Twain (1884);

in the early and mid-20th Century:

*Heart of Darkness* by Joseph Conrad (1902), *The Great Gatsby* by F. Scott Fitzgerald (1925), *The Sun Also Rises* by Ernest Hemingway (1926), *The Sound and the Fury* by William Faulkner (1929), *All Quiet on the Western Front* by Erich Maria Remarque (1929), *Rebecca* by Daphne duMaurier (1938), *Catcher in the Rye* by J.D. Salinger (1951), *On the Road* by Jack Kerouac (1957), *Lolita* by Vladimir Nabokov (1958), *Breakfast at Tiffany's* by Truman Capote (1958), *To Kill a Mockingbird* by Harper Lee (1960), *One Flew Over the Cuckoo's Nest* by Ken Kesey (1962), *A Clockwork Orange* by Anthony Burgess (1963), and *Cat's Cradle* by Kurt Vonnegut (1963);

and, in the last decades:

*The Color Purple* by Alice Walker (1982), *American Psycho* by Bret Easton Ellis (1991), *The Killing Floor* by Lee Child (1997), *Life of Pi* by Yann Martel (2001), *The Book Thief* by Markus Zusak (2005), *The Hunger Games* by Suzanne Collins (2008), and Janet Evanovich's novels featuring Stephanie Plum.

**Some of the advantages to writing your novel in first-person are:**

~ It mirrors real life – we experience life around us only from our own point of view – we don't know what other people are thinking. (Of course, you can get this same effect through close, intimate third-person POV or "deep" point of view.)

~ There's a direct connection from the narrator to the reader, so this POV can create an immediate sense of intimacy and believability.

~ The narrator-character's voice comes through more clearly, as it is expressed directly.

~ It's easier to portray the POV character's personality and worldview, as they're doing all the talking.

~ If your narrator is unique and appealing and you use lots of attitude and honesty in his relating of his story, you'll have a fascinating protagonist for readers to follow, with no distractions from other viewpoints like those of the author or other characters.

~ Advanced writers can try creating an unreliable narrator, one who's fooling himself as well as others. The gap between what he knows or believes and what is actually going on drives a lot of tension and intrigue.

**Some of the disadvantages of using first-person point of view and narration are:**

~ Too many sentences begin with "I" or have "I" in them. This can quickly become repetitious, tedious, and even annoying to the reader.

~ In the opening, the reader is often left wondering who "I" is. Be sure to mention your first-person narrator's name in the first paragraph or two, or certainly on the first page. A dialogue with someone else helps the reader figure out who this "I" is.

~ Working in a physical description of your protagonist can be a bit tricky, when we're in her point of view, and the looking in the mirror thing has been a bit overdone. (Again, close third-person point of view shares the same challenge.)

~ The viewpoint character has to be intriguing, with a distinctive, compelling voice, as we're "in his head" for the whole novel. As Morrell points out, "the first person is only as interesting as the character telling the story."

~ The reader may tire of the same voice and point of view predominating throughout the novel and feel that there's not enough variation in style and personality.

~ We may also get too much of the first-person narrator-character's opinions on people and events around him, and long for a little variety. How do the other characters see things?

~ There's a danger of too much introspection, interior monologue, and explaining things – in other words, "telling." Be sure to balance this with plenty of action and dialogue – "showing" – which will help the pacing and move the story forward more effortlessly.

~ With all those "I"s and "me"s, there's a danger of the writer putting too much of himself into the novel.

To work, your narrator-character needs to have a unique voice and personality, with lots of attitude. As James Scott Bell says in *Revision and Self-Editing*, "There must be something about the voice of the narrator that makes her worth listening to – a worldview, a slant, something more than just a plain vanilla rendition of the facts." On the other hand, don't make your narrator-character too weird, as that could get grating or annoying after a while.

In *The Successful Novelist*, Morrell discusses how he personally found first-person narration very suitable for short stories, "but I tried at least six of my novels in the first person, each time giving up in frustration once I got deeply into the story." He found it hard to overcome "the obvious liability of the first person, the nagging, narcissistic I-I-I of it." Morrell concludes, "Having been through this turmoil, I think I'll stick to using the first person only in short stories, while reserving the third person for my novels."

To circumvent some of the above problems, you can add multiple viewpoints to the mix. An alternative to using one first-person narrator for a whole novel could be to use first-person point of view for different characters, giving each character their own chapters, told directly by them, from their perspective. Even better (and less confusing, so preferable, I think), have your protagonist's viewpoint in the first-person using "I," then portray other characters in the third-person ("he" or "she") in their own chapters. Steven James uses this technique very effectively in his Patrick Bowers thrillers.

If you've written or started a book in first person, try rewriting a chapter or two in third person. Leave it for a few days, then reread the third-person attempt and see if you like the added freedom and variety of voice and viewpoint a little better. Or give both versions to a trusted friend or critique group and see which approach they prefer.

# Chapter 11 – Draw Readers in with Deep Point of View

In order to draw the readers in and engage them emotionally, make sure your story has a clearly dominant viewpoint character they can identify with and bond with. We should meet that main character (protagonist) right away, preferably in the first paragraph, and the first chapter should be entirely from her point of view, so the reader knows whose story it is and can start investing time and energy in her. When we experience the story through her, reacting as she does to her problems, it draws us into the narrative and we want to keep reading to find out what happens to her.

If we stick mainly with our protagonist, in his head and heart, without stepping back to describe things from the author's stance (omniscient POV), we're using deep point of view, or close third. When done well, this can be almost as intimate as first-person point of view. And it has the added freedom of switching to the villain's or some other character's POV (in their own scene) when it suits our purpose. Deep POV or close third-person viewpoint is a powerful way of engaging your readers quickly and making them worry about your hero right away, and keep worrying – which is precisely what you want.

One of the most difficult concepts for many aspiring fiction writers is to portray their story world through the viewpoint / eyes of one character at a time, rather than hovering above them (omniscient POV) or ping-ponging back and forth between different characters' viewpoints (head-hopping).

As Jack M. Bickham says in *The 38 Most Common Fiction Writing Mistakes*, "You'll never have problems with the technique of viewpoint again if you simply follow this advice: Figure out whose  story it is. Get inside that character – and stay there."

It's especially important to open your book in your protagonist's point of view, and stay there for at least the whole first chapter. This gives the reader a chance to figure out quickly whose story this is, and get to know him fast and start identifying with him and rooting for him.

Years ago I edited a novel that opened with a fifteen-year-old girl riding in a car with her mother, who's driving, and her eleven-year-old brother in the backseat. (I've changed the details a bit.) The book starts out in the point of view (thoughts) of the mom, who is worried about uprooting her two kids and moving across the country, away from their friends. So we start empathizing with the mother, thinking it's her story.

Then suddenly we're in the head of the teenage girl beside her, who is deeply resentful at her mom for tearing her away from her friends and agonizing over what lies ahead. Then, all within the first page, we switch to the head of the eleven-year-old boy, who's excited about the new adventure and wishes his sister would lighten up and quit hassling the mom. We're also in his visual POV – he looks at his sister's ponytail and considers yanking it.

Now we're confused. Whose story is this, anyway? Who are we supposed to be most identifying with and bonding with? Readers want to know this right away, so they can sit back, relax, and enjoy the ride.

Besides starting your third-person story in your protagonist's POV, it's also smart to tell most of the story from that character's viewpoint – at least 70 percent of it. In romance, the norm is probably more like 60% for the heroine and 40% for the hero, as a rough guideline. But definitely tell more than half of the story from your main character's point of view. That gets the reader deeper and deeper into that person's psyche, so they get more and more invested in what's happening to her.

As Bickham explains, "I'm sure you realize why fiction is told from a viewpoint, a character inside the story. It's because each of us lives our real life from a single viewpoint – our own – and none other, ever."

Successful fiction writers want their story to be as convincing and lifelike as possible, so they write it like we experience real life: from one viewpoint (at a time) inside the action.

So if you want your lead character to come alive and matter to the reader and your story to be compelling, it's best to show most of the action from inside the head and heart of your protagonist. Of course, thrillers often jump to the POV of the villain in another scene or chapter, to add suspense, worry, intrigue and dimension. But avoid going into his head in the same scene where we're in the hero's head. Also, make sure the antagonist is not onstage more than the protagonist is.

Many romances have two main protagonists, the hero and heroine, but the viewpoint of the heroine usually predominates, so the largely female readership can identify with her.

But don't be inside the head of both characters in one scene – that's too confusing. Or if you really want to show what the hero thinks of the heroine, switch the POV once only within a scene. A few best-selling authors like Nora Roberts are able to move seamlessly in and out of the viewpoints of their hero and heroine, but Roberts' scenes shown through only one viewpoint still seem more engaging to me. And when other, less experienced authors try head-hopping like this, readers often find it subliminally disconcerting, confusing, or annoying, even if they can't pinpoint what's bothering them.

Also, if there's a scene with your protagonist and a minor character, don't show the scene from the POV of the minor character, unless there's a very good reason for it – it's just too unnatural and jarring.

## So how exactly do we stay firmly in one character's point of view for a scene?

Perfecting this technique takes practice. Let's suppose you're writing a story about a macho, hero-type guy named Kurt, who defeats the villain, restores justice, and even gets the girl. It's Kurt's story so he's your main viewpoint character. How do you make sure your handling of his viewpoint is as powerful as it can be?

The first thing you need to do is imagine the setting, people and events as they would be perceived by Kurt, and only by him. As you write the story, you the writer must *become* Kurt. Or imagine you're an actor, playing Kurt. You see what he sees, and nothing more. You know what he knows, and nothing more. When Kurt walks into a bar, for example, you do not imagine how the bar looks from some god-like authorial stance high above, or as a movie camera might see it; you see it only as Kurt sees it, walking in purposefully and looking around.

And, of course, include his reactions to the other people in the bar. Show Kurt's feelings (and only his) about what and who he's seeing and his reactions to the situation. Instead of saying, "The bar was noisy, dark and smoky," say "The cigarette smoke in the air stung Kurt's eyes and, in the dim light, he couldn't make out if his target was there. As he looked around, the room started to quiet down. Heads turned, and eyes took him in, some curious, some hostile." This way, the reader is seeing the scene through Kurt's head and identifying with him, starting to worry about him. This from-the-inside-out approach is vital if you want your reader to care about your protagonist and get truly engaged in your story.

But you need to go even further – you need to describe what he's seeing and feeling by using words and expressions that he would normally use. If your character is a rancher or a drifter or a hard-boiled P.I, you're not going to describe the scene or his reactions in highly educated, articulate, flowery terms. Don't describe things he probably wouldn't notice, like the color-coordination of the décor, the chandeliers, or the arrangement of dried flowers in an urn on the floor.

It's also important to be vigilant that your viewpoint doesn't slip, so you're suddenly describing Kurt's reactions or facial expressions from the outside. Don't show us someone else's opinion about Kurt, or tell us about something that's happening out in the street or even in a hidden corner of the bar, while Kurt is still at the entrance of the bar. You can let the reader know other people's reactions to Kurt, not by going into their heads at this point, but by what Kurt perceives. He sees their disapproving, admiring, angry, curious, or intense looks, picks up on their body language, and hears their words and tone of voice.

Then, in a later scene or chapter, you can go into the bad guy's point of view and find out what he thinks of Kurt. Or, once he meets the girl, write a scene or chapter in her viewpoint so the reader finds out more about her and what she thinks of our hero Kurt.

This technique, properly used, will draw your readers effectively into your story world, where they really want to be, engaged, involved, and connected.

# Chapter 12 – How to Avoid Head-Hopping

In the last chapter, I discussed the effectiveness of starting out your story in your protagonist's point of view and staying there for most of the story.

**But how do we show the feelings and reactions of other characters?**

What if you want to reveal how other people besides the main character are feeling? If they're key characters, like the villain, a romantic interest, or a close friend or family member, you can give them their own POV. Create scenes where you get into their heads, and we see their thoughts, emotions, goals, aspirations and fears, as well as their physical sensations.

However, when other characters are in the same scene as your viewpoint character, you'll show their thoughts, feelings and attitude through what the POV character can perceive: their actions, words, tone of voice, body language and facial expressions. Say you're writing a romantic suspense or mystery, and you're in the heroine's point of view, showing her thoughts, perceptions and reactions. The hero, whom she's just met under unfortunate circumstances, is frustrated. You'll show his thoughts and reactions, not from inside him at that point (What the hell happened here?), but by what the heroine is seeing and perceiving – he glares at her, brows furrowed, runs his hand through his hair in exasperation, his body language is tense, his tone of voice shows his irritation, he's breathing fast, his words are abrupt, and so on.

The general rule of thumb is "one scene, one viewpoint." Or even better, wait for a new chapter to change the point of view to someone else's. If you change the perspective within a scene, it's best to do it only once, and leave a blank space before you start the next person's point of view. Ping-ponging back and forth can be jarring and confusing to the reader. This is what's referred to as "head-hopping." Some writers go so far as to leave three asterisks (* * *) and spaces above and below to indicate a switch in viewpoint within a scene, but I think that's too jarring and disruptive to the flow of action, since we're still in the same scene. Three asterisks, centered, are best reserved to indicate a shift in place and time.

## Why is it important to avoid switching viewpoints (head-hopping) within scenes?

When a reader becomes emotionally engaged in a book, it's like she enters right into the story and starts living it vicariously through the protagonist (viewpoint character). In order to fully enjoy the story, she chooses to pretend the story is real, to suspend her disbelief.

Every time you shift the readers from the thoughts of one character to another's, they're jarred out of their suspension of disbelief and reminded that they're only reading a story. Do that often enough, and they'll stop reading your story.

Here's an example of a viewpoint gaffe: Our heroine, Carole, is stirring the spaghetti sauce on the stove and talking to her husband on the phone. They're discussing the fact that their thirteen-year-old, Colton, is grounded. Suddenly, the author jumps into her son's head and shows Colton deciding to sneak out to meet his friends. He tiptoes past behind her back (his rap music is playing loudly in his room) and out the front door, then jumps on his bike and races off. Back to Carole, who continues to stir the spaghetti and talk on the phone.

What's wrong here? We were in Carole's POV, and she had her back turned so she wouldn't know Colton was sneaking past, especially with all that noise coming from his room. And how would she know he's riding away on his bike? Another jarring POV shift in the same scene would be if we suddenly started seeing her husband waving his secretary away because he's in an important conversation. We're in Carole's POV in this scene, and she can't see what her husband is doing at his office.

**Here are a few more examples of head-hopping. Can you spot the ping-ponging points of view? How can each scene be fixed to stay in one character's point of view per scene?**

Jerome drove along the country road, going over every detail of the meeting, trying to make sense of it all, as Sharon gazed out the window, reflecting on what had just happened and how it would affect their future.

What's wrong?

We're in the heads of both characters in the same sentence.

**Setup** – a scene in a shopping mall. We're in the point of view of Daniel, an off-duty cop who observes an attempted abduction.

As he strode toward the restrooms, Daniel bumped into a rough-looking, heavyset guy in a dirty jean jacket. "Oh, sorry."

"Asshole." The stranger glared at him and hurried on.

*Jerk.* As Daniel turned again toward the men's room, he dodged a young woman in her teens exiting the ladies' room. She was slim but curvy, wearing a tank top and shorts. Her searching eyes bypassed Daniel. It was clear she was looking for someone.

Two more steps brought Daniel to the men's room entrance, a feeling of ill-defined unease nagging at him.

Something felt off. He turned to watch the girl hurry away.

The scruffy man in the jean jacket noticed the young blonde girl and spun and headed after her.

When the man reached the girl, he moved beside her and draped an arm over her shoulder. He gripped her far shoulder with his left hand. With his right hand he pulled a handgun out from under his jean jacket, then displayed it before her startled eyes for a fraction of a second before pressing it to her ribs and clamping his left hand over her mouth. The girl's eyes grew

63

wide and instantly fearful as the man began to force her toward the exit doors.

What's wrong with the last paragraph above? Remember, we're in Daniel's point of view.

You got it – he's behind the man and the girl, so how can he see her startled eyes growing wide and looking fearful?

Perhaps show her tensing up and struggling instead, which would be easy for Daniel to observe from behind.

**Here's another one, about two twelve-year-old boys:**

Andy kept glancing up at the clock, waiting for the escape of the bell. The second hand moved around the clock with agonizing slowness until the dismissal bell finally rang.

Yay! The weekend at last! He ran out of the classroom, down the hall, and down the stairs to the exit.

His friend Josh stood at the foot of the steps waiting for him. Josh smiled as he watched his buddy Andy run down the stairs. Josh had moved to town a few months ago and still struggled to find friends. One recess they discovered they both loved baseball and had been inseparable ever since. Josh was so relieved to have a buddy to spend weekends with.

Andy raced down the last few stairs, eager for the weekend to start. When he got outside, he saw Josh and challenged him to a race. He took off. Josh watched Andy dart by, then ran hard, determined to catch up and pass him.

In the above scene, we're jumping back and forth between Andy's and Josh's viewpoints. Decide which character is the most important one for the story or that scene (which one has the most at stake), then start in the head of that character and stay there for the whole scene. Show the other character's reactions by what the POV character observes and perceives.

## HOW TO SPOT HEAD-HOPPING IN YOUR STORY:

My aspiring novelist clients find point of view one of the hardest fiction techniques to master. Here's a trick to clarify this concept for you and check for head-hopping in your story.

A quick way to check whose POV you're in is to get out the highlighters or colored pens and choose a different color for each of your main characters. Pick your protagonist's color, then start highlighting or underlining sentences that describe scenes, people, perceptions, and emotions strictly from her viewpoint – only details she can see, hear, or otherwise perceive. Do the same for other characters, with their color. When you're done, you should have paragraphs, and preferably scenes, of only one color. If you have another color creeping into that scene, see if you can rewrite those sentences from the dominant character's POV. If you have a number of colors within one scene, you've got some revisions to do. And as Stephen King says, "Writing is rewriting."

You'll find more POV slip-ups to solve in the appendix, "Spot the POV Gaffes."

# Chapter 13 – Tips for Using Point of View Effectively

Here are some guidelines, with examples, for avoiding head-hopping and other POV gaffes and getting deeper into the viewpoint of your character. These tips, of course, all apply to scenes written in third-person.

**First, decide whose scene it is.**

Most of the scenes will be from the viewpoint of your protagonist. We know what your lead character is thinking and feeling, as we're in their head and body. But we know the feelings and reactions of the others only by what they say and do and by their body language, facial expressions, tone of voice, etc.

But sometimes you'll want to write a scene from the point of view of another character. Make sure it's an important person in the novel, like the love interest, someone close to the MC, or the antagonist (villain). This is called multiple POV – but be sure to stick to the guideline, one POV per scene. This rule of thumb is sometimes broken in romances, where readers want to know how the hero is feeling too, what he's thinking and feeling about the heroine at that moment. But it's very difficult to do this well and seamlessly, so I strongly recommend one POV per scene, and leave an extra line space before switching to the other person's POV, then stick with that person's POV for the rest of the scene; or at the most, do one more switch back to the primary POV. Be sure not to ping-pong back and forth a lot.

How do you decide whose POV a scene will be told through? Ask yourself these questions: Who has the most at stake in that scene, the most to lose? Which character is invested the most in what's going on? Who will be most affected by the events of the scene and change the most by the end of the scene?

**Get into that character's head and body and stay for the whole scene.**

Don't get into the heads of others, and try to avoid stepping back into authorial (omniscient) POV, where you're surveying the whole scene from afar. Become that person for the scene. Are they cold? Uncomfortable? Worried? Annoyed? Scared? You can only see, hear, smell, taste, touch and feel what they do. Don't include any details they wouldn't be aware of.

Viewpoint shifts within a scene can be disorienting and mildly annoying if not done consciously and with care. On the other hand, when expertly executed, they can work. I'm currently reading a light romantic romp by Janet Evanovich and Lee Goldberg called *The Heist*, which has two protagonists who are opponents but attracted to each other. Chapter one starts out in the viewpoint of FBI agent Kate O'Hare and stays there for a while, to establish her as the heroine. Then, when she finally catches up with her target, the brilliant, handsome, and charming Nicolas Fox, we're suddenly in his POV watching her arrival. We stay there for a while until he cleverly escapes, then we're back in Kate's POV as she's frustrated, once again foiled by him. These accomplished authors manage the switch from Kate's POV to Nicolas's and back to Kate's within one scene quite seamlessly, without even using a space to indicate the switch in viewpoint. This technique works best for romances, where readers want to know how the love interest feels about the heroine.

**More tips:**

**~ When starting a new scene or chapter, start with the name of the POV character.**

The first name a reader sees is the person they assume is the viewpoint character, the one they're following for that scene. And don't start a new scene or chapter with "he" or "she" – that's too vague and confusing. When starting a new scene, we need to know right away who's head we're in.

**~ Refer to the POV character in the most informal way. Use the POV character's name at the beginning of scenes, then only when needed for clarity.**

If we're in Daniel's head, he's not thinking of himself as "Dr. Daniel Norton." He's thinking of himself as Daniel or Dan or Danny. When you introduce a new POV character for the first time, you can use their full name and title for clarity, but then switch to what they would call themselves or what most people in their everyday world call them. Most of the time, just "he" is even better. How often do we think of ourselves using our names? Not often.

**~ Don't describe the POV character's facial expressions or body language as an outside observer would see them.**

Unless she's looking in a mirror, your character can't see what her face looks like at any given moment, so avoid phrases like "she blushed beet red." Instead, say something like, "Her face felt hot and she knew she was blushing."

Or if we're in a guy's point of view and he's angry, don't say "His brow furrowed and he scowled." Instead, show his anger from the inside, or show him clenching and unclenching his fists or whatever.

**~ Refer to other characters by the name the POV character uses for them.**

And as the POV character gets to know them better, gradually take out their title, then last name.

Similarly, if we're in Susan's point of view and her mother walks in, don't say "The door opened, and Mrs. Wilson walked in." Say something like, "The door opened, and Mom rushed in, pulling off her coat."

## ~ Show their inner thoughts and reactions constantly.

To bring the character to life, we need to see how she's reacting to what's going on, how she's feeling about the people around her. Use a mix of indirect and direct thoughts. Short, direct thoughts are often in italics. For more on this, see the chapter "Using Thought-Reactions to Add Attitude & Immediacy."

## ~ Show their sensory reactions to their environment and others.

Use as many of the five senses as is appropriate to get us into the skin of the character. What is she hearing? Smelling? Are those sounds and smells pleasant or unpleasant? Or suspicious? Is she cold or too hot? Perspiring from nervousness? Cold and clammy from fear?

## ~ Describe locations and other characters as the POV character perceives them.

Filter descriptions through the attitudes, opinions, and preferences, of the viewpoint character, using their unique voice and speaking style. Don't step back and describe another character or a room in factual, neutral language.

## ~ Use only words the POV character would use.

If your character is an old prospector, don't use sophisticated language when describing what he's perceiving around him or what he's deciding to do next. Use his natural wording in both his dialogue and his thoughts – and all the narration, too, as those are his observations.

## ~ Don't suddenly have a character knowing something just because we as the readers know it.

If you're using third-person multiple POV, sometimes you may go into the head of another character, maybe the love interest or the villain, in their own scene, without the protagonist present. We readers know this other character by name, but the viewpoint character may not even know they exist. Later, we're in a scene in the POV of the main character when the secondary character appears to them for the first time. It's easy to slip up and use that character's name, since we know it so well, before the heroine and POV character knows it. Watch out for this subtle mistake creeping into your story.

~ **Don't show things the character can't perceive.**

Don't show something going on behind the character's back or in another room or location. Similarly, don't show what's happening around them when they're sleeping or unconscious. To do that, leave a line space and start a new scene in the POV of someone else. Avoid slipping into all-seeing, all-knowing, omniscient point of view.

~ **For even deeper point of view, try to avoid phrases like "she heard," "he saw," "she noticed," etc.**

Since we're in the character's head, we know she's the one who's hearing and seeing what is being described. Just go directly to what she's perceiving.

~ **Similarly, use "he wondered," "she thought," "he believed," and "she felt" sparingly.** Without those filter words, we're even closer in to the character's psyche. Go straight to their thoughts, beliefs, and feelings.

For practice using deep point of view or close third, see Appendix 1, "Spot the POV Gaffes."

# Chapter 14 – Psychic Distance

Steve Berry, in one of his workshops at Craftfest, the first two days of Thrillerfest, spoke about "psychic distance" – how close the reader feels to the various characters. These days, it's considered more effective to draw your readers in "up close and personal" to your protagonist, so they get more emotionally invested in him and his plight. That way, they feel compelled to keep turning the pages to find out what happens to him. Conversely, it's best to keep minor characters at an emotional distance proportionate to their importance to the story.

The following list shows ways to refer to your characters in your *Novel* book, starting way out in the distance in omniscient point of view, then gradually moving closer as the characters become more important to the story, until we're right in their heads, in close third POV, seeing and feeling what they are, reacting right along with them. This list is based on Berry's hierarchy, but expanded by me, with more details added.

*For novels*

Starting from furthest out and zooming ever closer in, refer to your characters as:

~ Generalities: person, people, kids, teenagers, men, women, office workers, moms, taxi drivers, police officers, man, woman, etc.

~ By their title or occupation: the detective, the police officer, the reporter, the cab driver, the waitress, the hotel clerk, etc.

~ Title plus name: Detective Jackson, FBI Agent Michael Smith, etc.

~ First and last name without job title or descriptor: Cotton Malone, Wade Jackson

~ Last name only – Malone, Jackson

~ First name only – Cotton, Wade

~ He, she, I (closest in)

Steve Berry will begin a book with the full name of his POV character, for example, Cotton Malone, to get us right into his head fast. He doesn't start with "the former Justice Department operative," as that's too distancing for the protagonist, whom we're supposed to identify with and bond with quickly. Then Berry immediately switches to just Malone, and works in later that he retired from the Justice Department. Berry doesn't use the full name again, as that would put us back at arm's length from the character.

Using their title as well as the name (Detective Wade Jackson) would back up the reader even more, and once we're in their head and the story is progressing, using the title alone ("the detective") would probably make the reader wonder who we're talking about.

But Berry takes it one step further and prefers to just use "he" most of the time when in Malone's viewpoint, to keep the psychic distance to a minimum. In this case, "he" is the equivalent of "I" in first-person point of view. For example, Berry uses Malone's name, then continues for three pages with just "he", until the beginning of the next chapter, where he starts with his name again. In another novel, Berry starts out with "Tom Sagan" (his protagonist), then switches to "Tom," then just uses "he" most of the time. As Berry says, "the tighter the psychic distance, the better it is."

You may not wish to take it this far, but do remember that if we're in a character's head, especially your protagonist, you don't want to use distancing descriptions of him or her like "the P.I." or "the doctor." It makes sense to start the novel with the full name and title, like "Special Agent Warren Cross" for clarity and to orient the reader quickly, but soon after, you'll likely switch to "Cross" (or maybe their first name) and stay there. If we've been in his head for a while and you suddenly refer to him as "the special agent" it will be very jarring to the reader, who may even wonder if another special agent has arrived on the scene.

Berry prefers to call female POV characters by their first name, and I tend to agree with him, for the most part. If the female is, say a police officer, in a milieu where everyone refers to each other by their last names, then use her last name when she's at work, and her first name when she's at home or among friends. In general, though, it seems more natural to call "close" female characters (and even most males) by their first name, especially when we're in their viewpoint. Along the same lines, Berry will usually refer to the villain by his last name, even in his POV, to create some psychic distance.

Using a related example, say your mid-20s male protagonist has hooked up with a female in her early 20s and they're on the run from the bad guys. Very soon, he's not thinking of her as "the grad student," or "the tall, thin girl" or whatever. As their bond increases, he's thinking of her only by her first name or "she." And to describe something they're doing, don't say "the two young companions" as again, that's too distancing. It reads like someone else talking about them, but we're in his head and he has become very close to her. He's not thinking of the two of them as "the two young companions." Just use "they" or "the two" or whatever.

On the other side of the coin, you definitely don't want to get into the point of view of any minor characters like store clerks, taxi drivers, and restaurant servers. In fact, it's best not to give them a name at all, unless they play a bigger role in the overall plot. Naming these walk-on characters can be distracting to the reader, who starts to think they have more importance somehow. So in general, stick with generic labels like "the cab driver," "the waitress," "the bellhop" or "the receptionist."

# Chapter 15 – Using Thought-Reactions to Add Attitude and Immediacy

In my editing and blog posts, I often suggest techniques for bringing characters and the scene to life on the page. One key method I advise over and over is to show the protagonist's immediate emotional, physical, and thought reactions to anything significant that has just happened. This glimpse into the POV character's real feelings and thoughts increases readers' emotional engagement, which keeps them eagerly reading

Showing your character's immediate thought-reactions frequently is a great way to let the readers in on what your character is really thinking about what's going on, how they're reacting inside, often in contrast to what they're saying or how they're acting outwardly. And it helps reveal their personality.

Here are some examples of brief, immediate thought-reactions:

> *Damn.*
>
> *In your dreams.*
>
> *What the hell?*
>
> *Give me a break!*

These direct thoughts, the equivalent of direct speech in quotation marks, are silent, inner words the character can't or doesn't want to reveal. It's most effective to italicize these quick, brief thought-reactions, both for emphasis and to show that it's a direct thought, like the character talking to herself, rather than the slightly removed indirect thought.

Here are a few examples of indirect thoughts vs. the closer in, higher-impact direct thoughts:

Indirect: She'd had enough. She really wanted to leave.

Direct speech: "I've had enough. I'm heading out."

Direct thought: *This sucks! I'm outta here.*

(Or whatever. More personal, more unique voice, more attitude, less social veneer.)

## Use present tense for direct thoughts.

If your story is in past tense, as most novels are, narration, indirect speech and thoughts will be in past tense, too. But it's best to put direct, quoted speech and direct, italicized thoughts in present tense, and first-person (or sometimes second-person), as they are the exact words the character is thinking.

## Direct thoughts = internal dialogue.

**Note:** Never use quotation marks for thoughts. Quotation marks are for words spoken out loud.

A few more examples:

Indirect thought: He wondered where she was.

Direct speech (dialogue): "Where is she?" he asked.

Direct thought: *Where is she?* Or: *Where the hell is she, anyway?*

Note how the italics take the place of quotation marks when it's a direct thought, the character talking to himself. Also, the italics indicate exact thoughts, so no need to add "he thought" or "she thought."

Indirect speech: She asked us what was going on.

Indirect thought: She wondered what was going on.

Direct speech: "What's going on here?" she asked.

Direct thought-reaction: *What on earth is going on?*

(Or whatever, according to the voice of the POV character.)

To me, using these direct thought-reactions brings the character more to life by showing their innermost, uncensored thoughts and impulses.

I advise against putting several long thoughts in a row into italics. In fact, do we even think in complete sentences arranged in logical order to create paragraphs? I don't think so. Thoughts are often disjointed fragments, as is casual dialogue.

Since italics are also used for emphasis, be sure not to overdo them, or they'll lose their power.

But do use italics for those brief, immediate thought-reactions, the equivalent of saying out loud, "What!" or "No way!" or "You wish." Or "I don't think so." Or "Yeah, right." Or "Great." Or "Perfect." Or "Oh my god." Only, for thoughts, take off the quotation marks, of course, so you'll write: *What!* or *No way,* etc.

To me, italics used in this way indicate a fast, sudden break in the social veneer, a revelation or peek into the psyche of the thinker.

So try to insert direct thought-reactions where appropriate to indicate your character's immediate internal reactions to events.

**But don't italicize indirect thoughts.**

To me, italicizing indirect thoughts (in third-person, past tense) would be the same as putting quotation marks around indirect speech, like: He said, "He wished he could come, too." (Should be: He said, "I wish I could come, too.")

So don't italicize phrases like: *Why were they looking for her? She had to find a place to hide!* ("Her" and "she" refer to the person thinking.)

Keep it in standard font:

> Why were they looking for her? She had to find a place to hide!

Some best-selling authors use a lot of italicized thought-reactions, while others use them sparingly or not at all. It appears to be a growing trend, though, and I think it's a great technique for highlighting the character's quick inner emotional reactions effectively, directly, and in the fewest possible words.

Lisa Scottoline, for example, uses italicized brief thought-reactions a lot in her novels. They provide a quick peek into the character's immediate thoughts, without a lot of explaining. Like in *Daddy's Girl*:

The heroine, Natalie, has a small cut on her face, and her father, on the phone, asks which hospital she went to. She says she didn't need to, "It's just a little cut."

> "On your face, no cut is too little. You don't want a scar. You're not one of the boys."
>
> *Oh please.* "Dad, it won't scar."

Later, a good-looking guy, Angus, makes a suggestion about lunch while they're working.

> *Did he just ask me out?*

Later, as they're working together, Angus tries to protect her, but she isn't having any of it. The thought-reaction shows the contrast between how she's really feeling and how she wants him to think she's going along with his plans.

> "I'll get you out of here in the morning, and you'll be safe."
>
> *No way.* "Okay, you've convinced me."

Andrew Gross uses frequent thought-reactions in italics very effectively in his riveting thriller, *Don't Look Twice*. Here's one brief example:

> A chill ran down her spine. ... *Don't let him see you. Get the hell out of here*, the tremor said.

And Dean Koontz uses this technique from time to time in his novel *Intensity*. For example, Chyna is hesitating about opening a door, then makes a decision.

> *Screw it.*
>
> She put her hand on the knob, turned it cautiously, and...

Then later:

> He was coming forward, leisurely covering the same territory over which Chyna had just scuttled.
>
> *What the hell is he doing?*
>
> She wanted to take the photograph but didn't dare. She put it on the floor where she'd found it.

Note that these intensified thoughts are often at the beginning of a paragraph or set off in their own line, for emphasis. Or sometimes they're at the end of a paragraph, to leave us with something to think about.

Lee Child's *The Affair* has lots of examples of Reacher's critical thoughts in italics. Here's one of many I could have chosen:

> He asked, "Was I on your list of things that might crawl out from under a rock?"
>
> *You were the list,* I thought.
>
> He said, "Was I?"
>
> "No," I lied.

(Not to nit-pick with a huge best-selling author, but in my opinion, neither the "I thought" nor the "I lied" are necessary above.)

Child also uses this technique a lot in *The Hard Way*, especially to show Jack Reacher's mind busily working away while he's talking to someone, or to emphasize the importance of a bit of info he's just learned.

David Baldacci uses this technique frequently in *Hell's Corner* to show the direct thoughts of his protagonist, Oliver Stone. Here's one example:

> *Burn in hell, Carter*, thought Stone as the door closed behind him.
>
> *And I'll see you when I get there.*

Brenda Novak, in her romantic suspense *In Close*, uses italicized thoughts to show the contrast between what the character, Claire, is saying and what she's really thinking:

> "Maybe I could get back to you in the morning after I've...I've had some sleep." *And a chance to prepare myself for what you might say....*

Finally, James Scott Bell uses this technique in his delightful novelette, *Force of Habit*. Sister J, a former actress and trained martial arts expert, is being confronted by someone obnoxious who has recognized her. Her internal dialogue shows her (unsuccessful) attempt at calming herself.

> "Can you still kick butt?"
>
> She could all right, and she felt like kicking something right now. His shin, if not the wall. *Think of St. Francis,* she told herself. *Think of birds and flowers...*

Short, italicized direct thoughts bring us closer in to the character. Be careful not to overdo them, though, as too many italics on a page can be distracting. And italics are generally used for emphasis, so readers will subliminally equate the two. Used in emphatic direct thoughts, they're perfect.

# PART IV

# SHOW VS. TELL – KNOW WHEN TO SHOW 'EM, KNOW WHEN TO TELL 'EM

# Chapter 16 – Show Important Scenes, Tell Transitional Scenes

"Show, Don't Tell." You'll hear this mantra a lot at writer's workshops and conferences and read about it in fiction-writing guides. Why? Because it's a critical concept to master if you want to engage your readers, get their heart rate quickening, and keep them turning the pages.

Nobody likes to be told about something second-hand. How often has your mind drifted when someone has launched into a lengthy story about something that happened that day, or recounted their European vacation, country by country? Or gotten into way too much detail telling you about a movie or a TV show or a book they've read? You want to take your own vacation or watch that movie or TV show or read that book yourself, not have it summarized for you second-hand, filtered through someone else's viewpoint, preferences, opinions.

Similarly, nobody likes to have an event in a story interpreted for them and to be told how they should feel about what happened. Readers like to experience scenes firsthand (or as if they were right there) and draw their own conclusions.

A common mistake among aspiring fiction writers is to *describe* or *narrate* (tell) significant events as if they took place at some point in the past. Instead, it's much more compelling to put the reader right in the middle of the action. Show the events as they occur, in real time, along with the characters' actions, reactions, inner thoughts and feelings, and actual words (direct dialogue in quotations). For a detailed introduction to this topic, see Chapter 3, "Show, Don't Tell," in *Fire up Your Fiction*.

**Showing brings your characters and scenes to life.**

So rather than describing and interpreting a critical situation, be sure to allow the reader the pleasure of "experiencing" it on their own by vicariously living it through a character who's interacting and reacting to what's happening.

Telling includes recapping scenes after the fact instead of showing them as they're unfolding. Telling also involves explanations to the readers and long, neutral descriptions, as well as going into lengthy detail on a character's background. All of these diversions interrupt the action and pull readers out of the pleasure and excitement of experiencing an event along with the characters.

Readers of modern fiction don't want to be kept at arm's length, to be told what's happening by an intermediary narrator. They hope to experience the events firsthand, to sense the character's fears, hopes, joys and worries and draw their own conclusions. They want to vicariously see what the character sees, hear what he hears, smell what he smells, touch what he touches, and even taste what he tastes.

It's in a scene with dialogue and action and reaction where your readers are truly engaged and excited. If you summarize critical events or have one character telling another about them after the fact, your reader will feel cheated, deprived of the pleasure and excitement of being right there to experience it as it happened.

Basically, you want to put readers right there in all the significant scenes, experiencing the action along with the POV character for that scene (most often the protagonist). Events are unfolding in front of us, just like in real life, and we're reacting to them (via the viewpoint character), worried about what's going to happen next, or angry at something someone else has said or done, or hopeful, or maybe even falling in love. But the outcome of the scene is uncertain, which is what keeps us reading.

When you show a scene, you use direct dialogue, thoughts, actions, and reactions. You stay in one character's head and body and

82

vividly show that character's internal and external reactions, his thoughts and his words. Do this for all major, pivotal scenes in your novel.

It's a lot easier to tell the readers that a character is feeling angry or bitter or sad or lonely than showing it. This is not only lazy writing but it's also imposing an interpretation, and readers will feel disappointed in your storytelling, often without realizing exactly why. *author's intrusion.*

**Why readers prefer showing rather than telling (whether they can articulate the difference or not):**

Whereas telling can feel patronizing or even condescending, like explaining things to the readers, showing respects the readers' intelligence, allows them the satisfaction of drawing their own conclusions.

**Telling is instructive; showing is entertaining.** Always keep in mind that the primary goal of fiction is to entertain. Any themes or morals should be alluded to subtly, through an entertaining story.

*No! To make a point (theme)*

**Showing involves the reader.** Showing lets the readers get directly involved. It makes your writing interactive, letting the readers play a part, too. Readers who are participating are engaged and committed.

**Showing engages your readers emotionally.** Showing evokes emotional responses in your readers, which is gold. *Telling just dictates to readers how they should feel,* which is deadly. So don't tell the readers your character feels sad or lonely or elated or angry or worried or frustrated – show it through their words, thoughts, reactions, and actions.

**Examples:**

*Telling:* She was embarrassed.

*Showing:* Touch [handwritten] Action [handwritten]

Her face felt flushed and burning. Her body broke out in sweat all over, and she sank low in her chair, averting her eyes, arms folded over her chest, wishing she could disappear on the spot.

Action [handwritten]

*Telling:* The biker looked scary.

*Showing:*

The Hell's Angels biker in black boots, leather pants, and a sleeveless black leather vest with fringes spat in the dust and revved his Harley Davidson. I tried not to stare at the stocky, barrel-chested man in his thirties with long, stringy hair, a shaggy beard, hard eyes, and a jagged scar running along his forehead. His nicotine-stained fingers gripped the handlebars, and graphic tattoos snaked up his thick, muscular arms.

*Telling:* The morning after getting struck in the head by a metal pole, I awoke with a splitting headache.

*Showing:*

> The next morning I could barely lift my head off the pillow. When I did, the bones near my left temple crunched. My cheekbones ached and my skull throbbed. **While I'd slept, someone had seeded the fold of my brain with red pepper and glass.**

~ from *The Moonlight Mile*, by Dennis Lehane (my bolding) There's more great stuff as the protagonist is trying to shower, but I'll let you read the book yourself.

## BUT SOMETIMES JUST TELLING IS BETTER

Of course, you can't show everything, or your book would be way too long, and it would tire your readers out – or worse, end up boring them. It's like reading someone's shopping list on Facebook – who cares! You don't want to show every move your characters make at down times, or when going from one place to the other.

That's where you summarize or "tell," to get them to the next important scene quickly, without a lot of tedious details.

If you have a minor, transitional scene, either delete most of it and replace it with a few sentences, or "tell" what happened through a brief summary, rather than showing it in all the details. For example, "They decided to take some time off to think it through. Three days later, they met to regroup." Then you start again with a "showing" scene, with dialogue and action and tension.

If it's a respite from the action, a recuperation scene, to analyze, regroup, and plan, go ahead and show it, if you like.

## CONCRETE TIPS FOR SHOWING INSTEAD OF TELLING

**Don't open your novel or short story with backstory on a character or telling readers about an earlier scene:**

Here's an example, well-disguised from my editing, of the opening paragraph of a short story. Here the author, through narration, reveals an important plot point by summarizing an earlier interaction.

> Due to some unforeseen medical bills and some uncooperative slot machines, Cliff owed a lot of money to an unsympathetic loan shark. The guy sent his big goon to knock Cliff around a bit, with a message: either pay up or end up in a dumpster. That afternoon, he sat in a sleazy bar on the dark side of town, dead broke, bumming beers off his best buddy and picking his brain for creative ways to get some money to pay off the debt. Unfortunately, all he could think of was being buried in garbage.

Although I really like the voice here, I think it would be more gripping, especially for a story opening, if both the scene with the goon and the scene with the buddy were dramatized, with dialogue, action, and reactions.

85

~ **Use mainly scenes with characters interacting,** with some tension and disagreement, with shorter "telling" transitions or reflective moments between these scenes.

~ **Show your characters in action**, and throw in plenty of immediate reactions, with conflict and tension.

~ **Cut way back on narrative description, exposition, and lengthy explanations** of the character's past (backstory) or the reasons behind their motivations.

~ **Don't tell readers how your characters are feeling.** Instead, show their *inner or outer reactions*.

*Before:*

> What's he pulling? What did he do with the money? Charles did not trust Parkins.

*After:*

> What's he pulling? What did he do with the money? *Damn the shifty bastard.*

~ **Don't tell readers how to feel.** Show them a scene with character actions and reactions, and let them draw their own conclusions and react as they wish. If your scene is vivid enough, it will produce the results you're aiming for.

~ **Keep flashbacks short**, have a good reason for each one, and show them in real time, with action and dialogue.

~ **Go for the concrete rather than the abstract, and specifics rather than generalities.** Tell what kind of vehicle, house, boat, dessert, flower, bird, fruit, etc. If a couple is celebrating their anniversary with dinner out, show the restaurant decor and what they're eating and drinking. And how they're dressed for the occasion. And of course how they're feeling. Show all the juicy details so readers feel they're right there too, seeing, hearing, smelling, touching, and tasting.

86

~ **Evoke all five senses.** Showing means presenting the story to the readers using sensory information. We, the readers, want to feel what the character is feeling, experience her fear, joy, anger, determination, and pain, and know her inner hopes and thoughts. We want to see what she's seeing, hear what she's hearing, smell the smells, feel the tactile sensations, and taste the food and drink along with her. Telling, on the other hand, is summarizing the story for the reader in a way that skips past the life-giving sensory information and just relates the basic actions and events that occurred.

**Some techniques for catching instances of telling and replacing them with showing**

~ **Look for places where you're *naming* emotions,** like *She was lonely. He felt angry. She found him attractive. Their honeymoon was the happiest week of their relationship.*

Instead, give specifics of why and how those emotions are manifested, and let the reader come to their own conclusion about how the character is feeling.

*Before:*

> The dead teenage hooker looked like she was sleeping, as if she'd wake up any minute. But she wouldn't. **Sadness enveloped Bateman.**

*After:*

> The dead teenage hooker looked like she was sleeping, as if she'd wake up any minute. But she wouldn't. *Jesus, she was just a kid. What a waste of a young life.*

~ **Do a search for "was" or "were" and rephrase many or most of the sentences, replacing the adjective with dynamic sensory imagery, including a compelling verb or verbal phrase.**

*Before:*

The pizza was delicious.

*After:*

Mushrooms and pepperoni formed colorful layers on the thick, bubbling mozzarella cheese spilling over bright red tomato sauce. We all grabbed slices simultaneously, the cheese stretching as we pulled our steaming triangles away. It was my first pizza in months, and I savored the familiar texture and every luscious taste. *Ahhh.*

~ **"He saw, he heard, he felt" puts a small barrier between us and the character.** Instead of saying *he saw* or *she heard* something, it's best to just show what they're seeing or hearing.

*Before:*

She heard and felt an explosion, then people screaming. She saw people running past the store. Then she heard sirens approaching.

*After:*

An explosion ripped through the air, making her eardrums hurt. Then screams, and people started running past the store, carrying young children. Sirens grew louder and more insistent.

~ **Instead of dialogue tags like "said angrily" or "asked anxiously," show the character's anger or anxiety through their words, thoughts, body language, etc.**

In this example, Janice, who desperately needs to find work, is in a job interview.

*Before:*

I'm assuming you can start tomorrow?"
"Yes," Janice said enthusiastically.

[What's enthusiastic about "Yes"?]

*After:*

"I'm assuming you can start tomorrow?"

"Absolutely." Janice leaned forward and smiled.

**~ Avoid telling after you've shown, just to make sure readers got it.**

*Before:*

*Is this really happening? Is he hiring me?* David **couldn't believe it** and spoke quickly. "I can handle anything you throw at me. I'm willing to do anything. If you give me a chance, I'll prove it to you." He couldn't mask the eagerness in his voice and hoped that he didn't sound pathetic **as he pleaded for this opportunity**.

*After:*

*Is this really happening? Is he hiring me? Yes!* David spoke quickly. "I can handle anything you throw at me. I'm willing to do anything. If you give me a chance, I'll prove it to you." He couldn't mask the eagerness in his voice and hoped that he didn't sound pathetic.

**~ No need to tell readers a character is asking a question:**

*Before:*

Kate took a sip of her coffee and **asked Jeannine another question**. "What do you think is really going on?

*After:*

Kate took a sip of her coffee and leaned forward. "What do you think is really going on?

**~ Even first-person narration needs showing, not telling:**

"I'm Doctor Suzuki. How are you feeling?"

89

I thought that was a dumb question. I felt like crap. I tried to answer, but couldn't, not even a growl. They had a drip hooked up to my wrist, and whatever it was had me doped up.

More specifics would be better here. Maybe something like "My head felt like it was about to explode and my mouth was like sandpaper. My brain felt like mush – probably from that drip they had hooked up to my wrist."

## ~ Show all critical scenes as they're unfolding

The main point to keep in mind is never to tell the reader, after the fact (or have a character telling another character), about a critical scene. Instead, dramatize it in the here and now, with dialogue, action, and lots of sensory details to bring it to life for the reader.

See the next chapter for more specifics on especially tense, edge-of-your-seat scenes.

# Chapter 17 – Critical Scenes Need Nail-Biting Details

When it comes to significant passages, don't skip over the details. Show every tiny movement, thought, and action. To increase tension, suspense, and intrigue, draw out crucial scenes – milk them for all they're worth.

Below are some "before" examples, well-disguised from my editing. In each example, including additional detail, including emotions, physical sensations, and reactions, would be much more effective in bringing the scene to life and keeping the readers on edge.

I've quickly created a possible "after" example for each one to illustrate what I mean, but I'm sure you can do even better.

**Setup:** Escaping from an insane asylum.

*Before:*

> Harley whispered, "I managed to lift the keys. Four in the morning. Get through the woods. I'll be waiting in a car on the other side."
>
> Jennifer didn't sleep at all that night. Four a.m. couldn't come soon enough. Harley had chosen that time because it was the morning shift change, when the attendants met to discuss what patient problems to look for. After they had settled into the cafeteria, Jennifer ran to the supply room that had an exit door at the other end. The keys worked perfectly, and she was out behind the hospital in less than a minute.

That was way too easy for suspense fiction. Nothing went wrong! Let's try that again:

*After:*

Harley whispered, "I managed to lift the keys to the supply room. Inside the room, there's an exit door that leads to the backyard. Do it at four in the morning. It's shift change, and they'll all be meeting to discuss the patients. Get through the woods. I'll be waiting in a car on the other side."

Jennifer didn't sleep at all that night. At four a.m., she threw on a robe and crept toward the supply room, flattening herself against the walls and ducking into doorways. She peeked around the last corner. *Damn.* An orderly was coming out of the supply room carrying towels. Jennifer ducked her head back and hid in a dark recessed doorway, clutching the keys so they wouldn't jiggle.

She heard footsteps approaching. She held her breath. The orderly passed, engrossed in his cell phone, so he didn't notice her. She raced to the storage room, glad she was wearing sneakers. Looking around, she tried one key after another, before finally hitting one that opened the door. *Yes.* She crept in and quietly closed the door behind her, then fumbled for the light switch so she could find the back exit. Just as she saw the exit straight ahead, she heard footsteps approaching. *Damn.* The orderly must be back. She snapped off the light and tiptoed toward the Exit sign in the dark. She fumbled for the doorknob and found it just as she heard a key in the other door. She yanked out the door and slipped out.

So far so good! But she still has to make it across the back field to the cover of the woods. And did the orderly hear her close the exit door?

Another "before" to continue the same story:

Jennifer looked around. It was pitch black and raining like crazy. With every step, she would sink a few inches into the muck, more walking than running. When she got to the edge of the yard, she searched for a hole in the hedge, then crawled

92

through. She hopped a barbed wire fence and saw a blue Toyota idling on the side of the road. She took off on a run.

My advice to the author of the original version was:

For nail-biting scenes like this, it's best to have more "showing" than "telling." Stretch it out a bit here for more trouble and tension and suspense. Also, amp up the tension by adding more danger and threats.

*After:*

It was pitch black and raining like crazy. And she was in her hospital gown. She started to run across the field, sinking into the muck with every step, more walking than running. Behind her, the door opened and a male voice yelled "Hey, you! Stop!"

*Crap!* She picked up her pace, glad she was away from the lights and there was no full moon. As she raced through the soggy field, the mud sucked off one shoe, then another. The alarm started blaring behind her. She limped along, bare feet sinking into the mud with each step.

When she finally reached the woods, she discovered that what from her window had looked like a thin hedge was instead a thorny knot of blackberry bushes. She ran along the edge looking for an opening. At last, she found an opening and crawled through. She hurried along the deer path for a while, then stopped. A barbed wire fence. *Damn!* She carefully grabbed the wires and pulled them up and down, then crawled through with difficulty. She could hear yelling and running behind her. She ran to the road and saw a blue Toyota idling there. She took off on a run.

Here's another example of adding details, emotions, and reactions to create a more riveting scene.

*Before:*

Linda opened the door of the tiny apartment.

Terry was gone, his clothes were gone, and so was the money. What! She ran down the concrete steps and into the parking lot. The Jeep was gone.

*After:*

Linda opened the door of the tiny apartment.

Where was Terry? She called his name. No answer. She surveyed the small room, then checked the bathroom and tiny bedroom. No sign of him. His clothes were gone too. *What the–?* Did he take the money, too?

Starting to panic, she searched under the bed and in the closet for the bag of cash. She yanked open all the dresser drawers and pulled out the contents, then ran and ransacked the small kitchen and living area. Nothing. *Shit!* The rat.

She ran down the concrete steps and into the parking lot. The Jeep was gone. *Christ.* Now what? She stomped her foot and ran a hand through her hair in frustration.

And one last example:

*Before:*

Ken ran down the back stairs. The wind was whistling between the buildings, and it felt like it was twenty below. He looked around for a car to steal and finally saw an old beater in the back of the parking lot. It wasn't locked, so he jumped in, hotwired it, and got the hell out of there.

It would be much more compelling to show the details of his struggle so the reader can picture what he's going through and get caught up in it, rather than skimming over and summarizing like this.

*After:*

Ken ran down the back stairs. The wind was whistling between the buildings, and it felt like it was twenty below. Hoodie up over his head, he darted through the parking lot,

94

trying one car door after another. All locked. *Damn!* He scanned the area and spotted a dented beater way in the back corner. He dashed over and tried the door. It opened. *Yes!* He jumped in, hotwired it, and got the hell out of there.

## But don't show details the character wouldn't notice.

On the other hand, skip any extraneous or distracting details, things the character wouldn't notice or care about at that critical moment.

Say your two characters, a young male and female, are on the run from bad guys in a large museum or art gallery. They'll be desperately looking for places to duck into or exits, concentrating on escaping alive. This is not the time to go into detail about the fascinating artwork or ancient artifacts around them. Perhaps mention a few in passing as they consider ducking behind them, or for some other reason relevant to their life-or-death situation. Describing their surroundings in detail is not only unrealistic; it dissipates the tension and slows down the pace at a time when they should be charging through at a break-neck speed.

In general, guard against showing too much detail in fast-paced scenes.

# Chapter 18 – How to Keep Your Dialogue Real and Riveting

Dialogue can make or break your story. Snappy, entertaining verbal exchanges can turn a good novel into an engrossing one. Stilted, flat, boring dialogue will sink a story, no matter how interesting the plot – because readers won't read past the first few pages.

Carefully crafted dialogue brings characters to life, differentiates them, and creates an authentic-feeling world for the readers. When the characters sound real, readers will trust the writer and allow themselves to get immersed in the story.

Convincing dialogue that fits the characters is one of the most challenging techniques for fiction writers to master. Often, conversation comes across as flat, expressionless, stilted, too formal, too correct, or all sounding the same, like the author.

Boring or stiff dialogue is an immediate turn-off for readers, agents, and acquiring editors, and sparking it up will immediately improve your story. Pay particular attention to the conversation in your first few pages, the make-or-break section where readers and agents will either keep reading or quit and turn to another story or manuscript.

Engaging dialogue propels the story forward at a good clip, adds much-needed tension and intrigue, reflects the character's age, gender, background, and education, and reveals their personality, attitudes, and mood. Remember that every character should speak differently, and not like the author.

Also, dialogue should not mirror real-life conversation, which is often mind-numbingly boring and repetitive. As best-selling author Dean Koontz says, "We read novels to see the mundane transformed into the splendid – not the other way around. ...Dialogue needs to be functional and entertaining."

As William Bernhardt so aptly puts it in *Dynamic Dialogue – Letting Your Story Speak,* "Dialogue is where your writing should snap, crackle, and pop. You need to get to the point without any messing about."

Look for the following dialogue sinkers in your fiction.

## DIALOGUE NO-NOS TO AVOID AND HOW TO FIX THEM

### Filler niceties

Leave out all the banal greetings and conversation fillers like "Hi, how are you?" "I'm fine," "Nice weather," and so on. Reality is no excuse for bad fiction.

### Monologues (info dumps)

Don't have one person going on for more than three or four sentences on a topic. Break it up with lively questions and answers. To keep the reader's attention, dialogue needs to be energetic, tension-filled, and compressed.

### AYKB – As You Know, Bob

This is where characters are telling each other things they both already know, in order to get that information across to the readers. This is discussed in more detail in my *Fire up Your Fiction* and in the chapter on avoiding author intrusions in this book.

### Overly formal, correct language with complete sentences

In casual conversation and especially in tense, heated interchanges, people rarely use grammatically correct, complete sentences. In your dialogue, break up complete sentences and use more casual expressions and slang. Replace formal words with more casual, everyday ones. Use lots of sentence fragments and one-word or two-word questions and answers.

### Everybody sounds the same, like the author

Make sure all your characters sound different. Of course, start by creating characters who are unique, even a bit quirky, and unlike you, for interest and contrast. Each character's word choices and speech patterns should reflect their age, gender, background, education, station in life, personality, and mood at the moment.

### Talking heads

This is where people seem to be talking, but we don't know where they are or what they're doing, and even the context is sketchy. Intersperse actions and action tags among your dialogue lines to situate the readers and supply information on the characters.

### "On the nose" dialogue

This is where everything is logical, and characters always respond directly to each other's questions. Instead, add tension and intrigue by using evasive responses, changes of topics, dissonant body language, gestures, or facial expressions, and even the odd lack of reply. Also, for added tension or to illustrate unresolved issues, try having your characters speaking at cross-purposes. Both are speaking, but neither is listening to the other.

### Not enough tension

All dialogue needs tension and conflict to keep it interesting. If your characters are agreeing, spark things up! Add questioning, subtle or overt disagreement, perhaps even some sarcasm, mocking, insults, or threats.

### Overusing names

Sure, we use each other's names occasionally in a conversation, especially if more than two people are involved, to make it clear which one we're speaking to. But we don't keep repeating the name of the person we're talking to, so be sure you don't overdo this in your dialogue.

On the other hand, when three or more people are talking, it's a good idea to use the name of the person being spoken to so it's clear who's being addressed. Also, when several people are talking, it's a good idea to name the speaker at the beginning of the line, to make it clear immediately who's speaking.

**Ridiculous regional dialects**

When trying to duplicate the speech patterns of people from specific regions, like the Deep South or Scotland or Australia, don't try to reproduce their accents phonetically. This can be annoying for readers who have to work to decipher the actual words. And it can also feel demeaning or insulting to people from that region. Just show the flavor and essence through choice regional words and expressions sprinkled in. For more on this, see Chapter 24 of *Fire up Your Fiction*.

## TECHNIQUES FOR DEVELOPING AN EAR FOR HOW DIFFERENT PEOPLE SPEAK:

Here are some tricks for developing your ear for authentic dialogue and internalizing the significant variations in speech patterns and expressions of people of different ages and in various walks of life.

~ Eavesdrop in restaurants, coffee shops, bars, parks, trains, buses, the subway, or other public places. Pretend you're reading or writing, but jot down snippets of conversation around you. Take note of the speakers' appearance and rough station of life to remind you later. Or record it surreptitiously on your cell phone, then play it back later in the privacy of your home.

~ If you don't get out much or you live in a remote area, try to watch a lot of TV shows or movies in your genre and pay close attention to the characters' words, expressions, and speech patterns.

~ Read aloud from best-selling stories in your genre. Role-play the dialogue with a friend or two. Reading great dialogue aloud will help you get the word choices and rhythm of different characters' speech patterns.

~ Use the internet to find screenplays of various movies or plays and study the dialogue. Again, read the parts out loud or role-play with a friend. You can also find collections of screenplays in books, for example, Best American Screenplays. Do a search for "screenplays" on Amazon.

## QUICK WAYS TO IMPROVE YOUR DIALOGUE

~ **Break up monologues** – one person going on for too long explaining something to someone else. Use questions and answers instead, preferably with a bit of tension. And ask yourself if some of the info can be omitted. Remember, this is fiction, not nonfiction, and if readers want to know more about the subject, they can always Google it.

*Before*:

Who are the Peshmerga?" questioned Victor, unfamiliar with the name.

"The Peshmerga represent a group of armed Kurdish resistance fighters trying to win their independence from Saddam Hussein. They want to help us. Our problem lies with the fact that the Turks and Kurds don't trust each other having tribal conflicts extending back for centuries. Right now, our diplomats are working to persuade the Turks to allow our pre-invasion build-up at several of their bases, and the negotiations have stalled as the Turks' loyalty is with the other Muslim countries of the Middle East.

*After*:

Who are the Peshmerga?" asked Victor.

"They're armed Kurdish resistance fighters who are trying to win their independence from Saddam Hussein. They want to help us. Problem is, the Turks and Kurds don't trust each other. Their tribal conflicts go back centuries.

"So where do the Turks come in?"

"Well, right now, we're trying to persuade the Turks to allow our pre-invasion build-up at several of their bases, but the negotiations have stalled."

"Yeah? Why's that?"

"The Turks' loyalty is with the other Muslim countries of the Middle East, not us.

~ **Make sure most of your dialogue uses casual language and everyday words.**

Read your dialogue out loud to see if you can make it (and also thoughts and narration) flow more smoothly and sound less stilted and more casual and natural.

Disguised from my editing of crime fiction, two cops who work together and know each other well:

*Before*:

"There's been a break in the case."

"Already?"

"Yeah. We got a response concerning the APB the department sent out to all law enforcement agencies in the Tri-State area. They found the black SUV in the Bronx."

"That was fast. Now let's get the paperwork initiated and completed so that we can have the SUV brought back to the precinct for processing."

*After*:

"There's been a break in the case."

Already?"

"Yeah. We got a response from the APB the department sent out to the Tri-State area. They found the black SUV in the Bronx."

101

> "That was fast. Let's get the paperwork done so we can get the SUV back to the precinct for processing."

And another example:

*Before*:

> "Do you have anything better you can think of?"
>
> Mike wanted to answer yes, but his mind reeled, overwhelmed with information.

*After*:

> "Do you have any better ideas?"
>
> Mike wished he did, but his mind wouldn't stop reeling.

Here's another conversation between two men who know each other well:

*Before*:

> "What happened then?"
>
> "I gave him copies of all the research papers with the exception of the key document. I hadn't even looked for it but I lied and told him I couldn't find it. I was stalling while I tried to devise a way to stop him."

*After*:

> "What happened then?"
>
> "I gave him copies of all the research papers except the key document. I didn't even look for it, but I lied and told him I couldn't find it. I was stalling while I tried to figure out a way to stop him."

And even for a relatively formal interaction, go for smoothness of delivery:

*Before*:

> "Who are you choosing to lead the assault?"

"Trevor, sir. He has demonstrated exemplary leadership and service. I believe the mission necessitates his promotion."

*After*:

"Who are you choosing to lead the assault?"

"Trevor, sir. He has demonstrated exemplary leadership and service. I believe he's essential for the success of the mission."

## ~ Use action tags to avoid "talking heads."

Situate your readers with little action phrases among the quoted dialogue to replace some (or many) instances of "he said" and "she said" Use characters moving about, picking up and putting down objects, leaning back or forward, rubbing their eyes, etc. How much detail you include on characters' actions depends on the pace you're going for in that scene. If it's a tense scene, short, staccato dialogue with few action tags is more forceful. If it's a more leisurely passage, include more character actions. But do be sure each action beat has some relevance to what's going on, and isn't just there as filler, which can be distracting and even subliminally annoying.

Here's an example of effective action tags to replace speaker tags, from *The Trap*, by L.J. Sellers:

"I nearly peed my pants!" He practically vibrated with energy.

Dallas felt a little giddy too. "An usher ran me off, but I circled back. The whole thing was surreal."

Abby laughed at both of them. "You think that was nerve-racking? Wait 'til you hear what we have planned next."

"What?" Dallas pulsed with eagerness to know.

"Not yet. We'll talk at the meeting."

## ~ Use subtext, hints, allusions.

To add interest and tension, include the odd suggestion of feelings that are below the surface, perhaps the opposite of what the character is saying. Have the characters responding in strange ways that arouse curiosity and questions. Maybe readers are aware of the subtext but the other character isn't, or this is the first indication to the readers that something is amiss, or things aren't as they appear on the surface. Subtext can allude to previous relationships, previous arguments, wrongs, secrets, sources of tension or conflict, and so on.

## ~ Finally, be sure to make the dialogue of kids and teens sound like real kids.

Don't choose words young people of that age are unlikely to say in that situation. Sometimes, minor tweaking can make the difference. Have kids in your life read those parts out loud and tell you where it sounds off. Anywhere they hesitate or stumble is a good indication that the language needs to be relaxed. On the other hand, exercise caution when using the latest slang expression, which could quickly date your novel.

# PART V

# IMMERSE THE READERS IN YOUR STORY WORLD

# Chapter 19 – Make Sure Your Characters Act in Character

## Do your characters' decisions and actions seem realistic and authentic?

Have you ever been reading a story when suddenly the protagonist does or says something that makes you think, "Oh come on! Why would he do that?" or "This is crazy. Why doesn't she...?" or "But I thought he...!" or "I didn't know he/she could [insert extraordinary ability]." The character seems to be acting illogically, to be making decisions with little motivation or contrary to his personality, capabilities, or values. *Must 1st. show motivation. What is leading the char. to do/say what he/she does says*

I see this problem a lot in fiction manuscripts I edit. The author needs something to happen for the sake of the plot he's planned out in advance, so he forces a supposedly intelligent character to do something contrary to common sense and her best interests, like recklessly putting herself in danger. *Don't want an illogical action*

For example, I once edited a book where the highly educated, intelligent heroine rose from her bed in the middle of the night and, without telling her husband where she was going or even leaving a note, drove to a remote warehouse to find some incriminating evidence, knowing the killer was likely to return – which of course he did, and attempted to kill her. It made for an exciting scene, but unfortunately, the otherwise savvy character came off looking like a foolhardy, impulsive airhead. I couldn't help wondering, why wouldn't she tell her husband? Better yet, call the police and let them handle it. Even police, who are trained for these situations, usually get backup.

*Must show motivation 4 Char's behavior or might lose readers if they cannot see the plausibility of the char's behavior.*

Moving your characters around like pawns to suit the plot, if it doesn't make sense, for who they are, could have your readers scratching their heads in disbelief or, worse, throwing your book across the room, then writing a scathing one-star review of it.

**Don't force your characters, kicking and screaming, into actions they just wouldn't do.**

Readers won't suspend their disbelief and bond with the character if they don't "buy" what the character is doing and why. An engrossing story needs realistic characters dealing with adversity in bold but authentic, plausible ways. *They have to relate to the chars.*

To make a character's decisions and actions convincing, take care when creating their background, character, abilities, and motivations.

**Background, character, and personality** *For me, can be all these ways.*

*ild bride*

Of course, you don't want to make your hero or heroine ordinary, timid, or passive, with few daring decisions, because that would make for a ho-hum book most readers wouldn't bother finishing. But on the other hand, if you're going to have them perform daredevil feats, be sure to build that into their makeup.

First, get to know your main characters well. Take some time to develop their background, character, and personality. Are they athletic or more cerebral? Risk-takers or cautious? Do they embrace change, enjoy challenge, love to learn new things? Or do they prefer to stay within their comfort zone? To plumb their depths, do some free-form journaling or put them on the psychiatrist's couch, where they express their strongest desires, fears, hopes, secrets, regrets, and gripes.

Are they physically capable of what you want them to do?

**Abilities**

If, for a riveting plot, you need your hero to do something heroic, almost superhuman, make sure he has the determination, strength, flexibility, and endurance to do that. Although it's amazing what people are able to do under duress with the adrenaline flowing, it's more credible if your character is already at least somewhat fit. Does he work out a lot to maintain muscle mass, agility, and endurance? How? Also, he'll need to be intelligent, skilled, and resourceful.

If he needs special skills, show earlier on that he possesses them and how it all makes sense, given his overall makeup. In one novel I edited, the sedentary, slightly overweight, middle-aged protagonist fought off a strong attacker with quick, expert martial arts moves. This was an "Oh, come on!" moment, given his lifestyle, age, and paunch.

*Dimensions – Round char.*

In *The Hunger Games*, we learn early on that Katniss is an expert at archery, which is a key factor in her survival later. A nerdy banker probably doesn't do kickboxing on the side, so you may need to make him less desk-bound and more athletic for it to work. Or give him another profession.

If you're writing fantasy, of course you have more leeway with unusual characters and situations, but if you're writing a realistic genre with no supernatural or paranormal elements, make sure the character's actions are credible and make sense.

## Motivations

Is your hero sufficiently motivated to put his life on the line? Do those motives fit with his belief system, background, and immediate needs? If you want or need a character to do something dangerous, go back and give him some burning reasons for choosing that course of action.

Perhaps he finds himself in a life-and-death situation for himself or someone he loves, or innocent people are in grave danger. His love, concern, and determination will make him more selfless and daring, bringing out courage he never knew he had.

*Students write one way in class and then suddenly come to class holding a paper with a completely diff. style, I would wonder whether the stud. plagiarised.*

108

As Steven James advises in *Story Trumps Structure*, as you're writing your story, ask yourself, "What would this character naturally do in this situation? Is he properly motivated to take this action?"

## Causality

Be sure your narrative is also shaped by the logic of cause and effect. For your story to be believable, character decisions and reactions need to plausibly follow the original stimulus or actions. If your character overreacts or underreacts to what has just happened, they won't seem "in character" or real.

Be sure every decision and action makes sense with what preceded it. As James suggests, as you go along, continually ask yourself, "What would naturally happen next?"

So don't force your characters to act in uncharacteristic ways because your plot needs them to. Readers will pick up on that. Rather than insisting certain events or actions happen as you had planned, instead allow the natural sequence of events and logical reactions to shape your plotline.

Go through your story to make sure your characters are acting and reacting in ways that are authentic to who they are and where they've come from, and that they're sufficiently motivated to take risks. Also, do their reactions fit with the stimulus? Is that a logical response to what happened?

Ask yourself, as you're writing, "Is there a way to accomplish this that fits with the character's values and personality?" If not, I suggest you either change the plot (have them make a different decision and rewrite where that leads them) or go back and change some of the character's basic attributes, values, and skills. Or add in incidents in their past that have shaped them in ways that will justify their current actions.

Char. can't be walking forward + backward same time. Intelligent readers will say his is balony – tommyrot.

109

That way your plot will flow seamlessly, and your characters will seem real. There will be no bumps, no hiccups where readers will be jolted out of the story.

As William Faulkner advised one of his fiction-writing classes,

> "...get the character in your mind. Once he is in your mind, and he is right, and he's true, then he does the work himself. All you need to do then is to trot along behind him and put down what he does and what he says."

So don't impose your preconceived ideas on the character – you risk making him do things he just wouldn't do. Know your character intimately, *be* your character, and the rest will naturally follow.

# Chapter 20 – How to Avoid Annoying Author Intrusions

**What is author intrusion and why is it (subliminally or overtly) annoying to readers?**

When readers pick up a novel or short story, they're hoping to escape their cares or humdrum lives and get swept up in an exciting story. They want to vicariously experience the story world through an intriguing lead character. Ideally, for maximum escapism, they will almost *become* the character for the duration of the novel, to see and hear what the character sees and hears, from her unique viewpoint, slanted by her personality, opinions, and attitudes. Readers don't want someone else (the author) butting in to clarify points or alert readers of details outside the character's perception and knowledge. That's heavy-handed and can feel manipulative and controlling. Not to mention it's obvious and clunky.

So to maintain your story's magic, to keep readers immersed in the fictive dream, it's important not to jolt readers out of it by butting in as the author to explain things or to soapbox about your pet peeves or social issues.

Author intrusions can range from blatant instances of the author barging in to alert readers or expound on a topic, to subtly (or not so subtly) expressing her opinions through the characters, to the even more subtle (often inadvertent) sprinkling in of words and terms that person likely wouldn't use, given his background, education, gender, and personality.

These careless intrusions jolt the readers out of the story and remind them that they're just reading a book. Or they may feel the author is trying to shove his opinions down their throat. They may put the story aside and not pick it up again, without analyzing exactly why they've lost interest.

Not only do author intrusions distract and annoy readers, they also shout "amateur" to agents and acquiring editors. They indicate a developing writer who still has a long way to go to succeed in today's competitive world of fiction writing.

## BLATANT AUTHOR INTRUSIONS TO AVOID

**~ The author interrupting the narrative to address the readers directly about anything.**

For example, in a historical fiction, the author interrupts to enlighten the readers: "In those days, it was commonplace to..." or "Back then, people didn't realize that..."

Or, in a contemporary fiction, when we're in the main character Rick's head and viewpoint, the author tells us as an aside, "Little did Rick realize that the killer was watching him from..."

These types of author intrusions were common in past centuries, but are usually considered intrusive by today's readers, unless it's a parody of some kind or done in a humorous way, like the children's Lemony Snicket books.

**~ Lecturing or preaching**

This is when the author's agenda is blatantly evident because she's constantly trying to convert the readers to her pet causes or sway them to her political, social, or religious beliefs. Even if it's done in the guise of a character's opinions, if it's too blatant or strident, readers will feel manipulated and start to distrust the author and lose respect for her.

If you really want your novel to have a moral, show it through character interaction, dialogue, and consequences — but be subtle about it. Don't have one character lecturing another on a topic or moralizing about an issue. Instead, show the adverse effects of harmful behavior through character choices and unfortunate consequences. For example, teenage boys who've been drinking decide to drive anyway and end up crashing the car, causing severe injuries or even death. That would be much more riveting than having one of their fathers lecture them about the dangers of driving while under the influence of alcohol or drugs.

## ~ Information dumps

The author has spent so much time researching a topic that he feels compelled to include most of his research in the novel to justify his efforts. He forgets that, unlike nonfiction, where the goal is to impart information to readers, the main purpose of fiction is to entertain and enthrall. In most genres of fiction, it's best to include only the information that is needed at that point to avoid confusion, and leave the rest out. And be sure to present it in a natural way, through dialogue with spark and tension.

In historical fiction, readers want a feel for the times depicted, but they don't want lengthy history lessons. Rein yourself in. Remember, if they're really interested, they can easily do a Google search to find out more. Savvy authors will do their research so they're on solid ground and their knowledge will ensure an accurate portrayal of the times, but most of the information stays out of the novel.

For example, in Dennis Lehane's *Moonlight Mile*, we find out details of the history of the Russian mafia, but in a natural way, through dialogue, not as the author interrupting the story to explain it to us.

"What's to stop him....?"

"His word that he wouldn't is all I got to go on."

"And you'd take it – the word of an assassin who goes all the way back to the Solntsevskaya Bratva in Moscow?"

"I don't even know what that is," I said.

113

"A gang," she said, "a brotherhood. Think the Crips or the Bloods with military discipline and connections going all the way to the top of the Russian oil conglomerates."

"Oh."

"Yeah. That's where Yefim got his start. And you'll take his word?"

### ~ Description dumps of scenery and other setting details

Don't describe the setting in great lyrical detail, from a neutral point of view, as the author. This is fiction, not a travelogue. Readers tend to get bored with description quickly and (if you're lucky) will skip past it to get to the action. Details you include should be relevant to the encounter, enhance the mood and tone, and reflect the character's attitude, opinions, and physical sensations.

If a character is under stress and running for his life through the woods, he's not going to be thinking about the gorgeous fall colors, the burbling brook, the scampering squirrels, and the birds singing! He's more worried about avoiding noisily thrashing through the woods or tripping over rocks or roots and falling. His primary focus is evading his pursuers, so he'll only notice critical aspects of his environment.

Or if your character is in a similar situation in the city, she won't be admiring the architecture or the reflection of the lights in the puddles. She'll be focused on how to escape her pursuers. Besides being out of character and inappropriate for the circumstances, "travelogue" type details destroy the tension that is critical in these kinds of scenes.

### ~ Overdescription or neutral, "listing" depiction of characters

This is where, when a new character comes on the scene, the author interrupts the action to give a laundry list of his height, build, hair color, eye color, and everything he's wearing. This kind of portrayal is not compelling and doesn't take into account the impressions and feelings of the character who's observing him, which is vital.

Similarly, don't use words and expressions to describe the new character that the POV character observing him wouldn't use, or mention features they wouldn't notice or care about. (See below for an example of this.)

## ~ Backstory dumps

This is where the author interrupts the story to tell readers unnecessary and even irrelevant details about that character's recent or childhood background. Newbie fiction writers mistakenly feel that readers need to know a lot about each new player as he is introduced. Stopping to fill us in on the character's history is intrusive and annoying. Instead, mention relevant details bit by bit through dialogue or thoughts, only where they make sense and tie in to what's happening at that moment.

Hinting at critical information but holding back on the details also increases intrigue and reader curiosity, compelling them to keep turning the pages to find out more.

## ~ Dialogue dumps

Intrusive background information can take the form of "dialogue dumps," where the author decides to have a character pontificate on a topic or preach about a social issue or pet cause to another character. Real people won't put up with this from their friends or colleagues, so your characters shouldn't be doing it either. And readers could easily interpret it as an attempt to convert them to your point of view, impress them with your knowledge, or instruct them on a topic they can easily research online if it interests them.

A specific kind of dialogue dump is the **"As You Know, Bob" (AYKB)** phenomenon, an obvious sign of amateurish writing where characters rehash information they both know, for the benefit of the readers. Here's a rather extreme, amusing example, which was recently making the rounds on Facebook.

Mary and Claire sat down at their favorite table at their favorite restaurant. "As you know, Claire," said Mary, "we've been coming here every Sunday for the past twenty years."

Claire nodded. "Yes, and ever since my husband Steve had that heart attack three and a half years ago, leaving me enough money to pay off the mortgage, I've been able to buy us lunch."

Mary shook her head sadly and gave her friend a gentle smile. "Unlike my husband Rick, who, as you know, had a terrible boating accident in 1983, your Steve was wise with his money."

Claire nodded her agreement. "And thank God for that wisdom of his. We wouldn't have ever been able to open that orphanage up to the homeless, abused children of San Francisco the way we did without my dead ex-husbands good business sense."

"It's true," agreed Mary. "And we've been running it successfully for over ten years now!"

People don't reiterate their past at a casual lunch with a close friend. Especially when they're discussing facts they both know well. Even if you have a dialogue that is much less obvious than this one, ask yourself if those characters would actually speak to each other that way.

But how do we sneak critical background info in naturally, as the characters would actually speak? You can use brief internal narration (thoughts). But be sure to stay in the character's voice and POV.

Another effective way that rings true and adds tension is through an argument or confrontation, where each person is bringing up past wrongs or faults, flinging accusations:

"Yeah? What about last summer when you...?"

"I'm not the only one who... Remember that time you..."

116

## ~ Flashback dumps

This is where the author inserts a lengthy and unnecessary flashback to the past. Go ahead and add in brief flashbacks here and there if you wish, but make sure the information revealed is critical to the story line or contributes details that impact the character's present motivations and decisions. If it's just to show a general background situation with everyday facts, leave it out.

And be sure to show your flashbacks in active scenes with dialogue and action, rather than as "telling." Don't have the person sitting there relating a story from the past. Take the readers directly to the scene, where they can hear and see and feel along with the character as the scene unfolds.

## ~ Amateurish foreshadowing

This is when the author says something like, "As Eve got off the bus and hurried to her apartment in the dark, she didn't see a dark figure step out of an alley, flip up his hood, and start following her." This is the author pushing the character aside and butting in to alert the readers of something that's going to happen or something out of the character's awareness, a clear attempt to increase tension and intrigue. This shatters the fictive dream and jolts us out of our immersion.

Plus it would add delicious tension and intrigue to have Eve hear footsteps approaching behind her and start worrying about who it could be.

Another example would be, "Jim quietly jimmied the lock and entered the suspect's house. As he tiptoed along the hall, little did he know that upstairs an attacker waited silently, gun drawn."

## MORE SUBTLE AUTHOR INTRUSIONS TO WATCH FOR

**~ Terminology and expressions that don't fit the era or geographical region.**

Writers of historical fiction need to be especially vigilant to not let today's trendy expressions creep into their depiction of life a hundred or two hundred years ago. I once edited a historical fiction set in the 1800s where the author used the terms "upscale neighborhood" and "high-end shops," both expressions coined within the last 50 years. (According to Merriam-Webster's dictionary, *upscale* was first used in 1966, and *high-end* wasn't used until 1977.)

Similarly, a Brit's car has a "boot" and a "bonnet," while in North America we call them the "trunk" and the "hood." What Americans and Canadians call a "sweater" or "pullover" is called a "jumper" in the U.K. "Cookies" in North America are "biscuits" in the U.K., and "chips" are "crisps." Canadians wear "tuques" to cover their heads in cold weather, whereas Americans call them knitted caps. Be sure to do your research and use terms and expressions those characters would actually use in that environment and particular situation.

To prevent these anomalies, be sure to find beta readers who have lived in the geographical region where your story takes place.

**~ Characters using words and phrasing that are "out of character" for their age, background, education, and personality.**

Little kids playing in the park or woods aren't going to know the names of all the flora and fauna, for example. Nor do they care – they're busy playing hide-and-seek!

Or, as occurred in a story I edited, a character the POV character meets for the first time is described using trendy fashion terms the down-to-earth detective would never use or think. This is in the POV of a tough, harried police detective investigating a murder in a theater.

> Powell asked to speak to the manager. The tall, slim theater manager came out of his office wearing the latest in hipster couture. He was decked out in a slim-fitting one-

button hounds-tooth blazer, custom-tailored skinny jeans, and Italian loafers. As a finishing touch, he wore a beautifully knotted silk scarf around his slim neck.

I can't imagine that hard-nosed detective thinking in terms of "hounds-tooth blazer" and "beautifully knotted silk scarf." With a little effort, you can still convey the impression that the manager was stylish or affected, but from the character's viewpoint, not the author's.

~ **Generally formal or "correct" language for character dialogue, thoughts, or narration.**

Avoid grammatically correct, complete sentences and also words like "whom," "therefore," "however," "nonetheless," and "subsequently" in casual dialogue and thoughts; for example:

*Before:*

> Katie grabbed her cup and headed to the kitchen for a refill and some breathing space. My whole life is out of control, she thought. What am I going to do, whom can I trust? I don't seem to know anyone around me anymore, or maybe, she chided herself, maybe I never did.

"Whom" is too formal for informal dialogue or a person's inner thoughts, especially when they're upset. Here's a more informal version of the above:

> Katie grabbed her cup and headed to the kitchen for a refill and some breathing space. Her whole life felt out of control. *What am I going to do? Who can I trust?* She didn't know anyone anymore. Or maybe – maybe she never did.

~ **Suddenly Superguy – a character has specialized knowledge, skills, or talents.**

The author wants or needs something to happen so he forces a plot point or character decision or skills that aren't organic to the

119

character. For example, to get out of a fix or escape the bad guy, a character suddenly has special powers that haven't been mentioned earlier in the story. Perhaps the character has detailed knowledge of subjects he is unlikely to know about, or unexplained talents or skills. For example, your average office worker thrown into a dangerous situation probably doesn't know much about picking locks or fighting bad guys or defusing bombs or dealing with serious injuries. Either show him bumbling or somehow establish how he would know this before this day. Has he carefully watched a lot of TV shows on the subject? Has he taken a first-aid course? Is he secretly taking Taekwondo lessons? If so, why?

**~ No distinct personality or voice. All the characters sound like the author.**

All or most of the dialogue and narration sounds the same, neutral, or like the author speaks and thinks. Male characters use phrasing and word choices that could easily be those of the female author, or vice versa. Each character's speech patterns should be unique and should reflect their age, gender, education, and background, as well as their personality. This is especially critical for kids.

**~ Backstory details inserted into the narrative for no apparent reason.**

Suddenly we're in the character's past and we have no idea why. Be sure there's an incident of some kind that sparks the character's memory and makes him think of something in the past. It could be a running into an old acquaintance or an offhand comment, a favorite location, a song from the past, or a scent that sparks memories.

**~ Backstory inserted at the wrong moment or that doesn't fit the situation or the stimulus.**

Carole is interviewing for a job, a position she really wants, so she's eager and nervous.

The CEO said, "This position will entail a lot of extended travel. Do you have responsibilities here? A husband and kids? Pets?"

Carole leaned forward. "No, I'm divorced and I have no kids." She and Paul had met while in college and, after dating for two years, married when they both graduated. They had hoped to start a family but he was away a lot on business, and they started drifting apart. They didn't have that much in common, as it turned out.

"We need someone right away for this position. When can you start?"

"I'm available now, sir. I could start today or tomorrow."

The details of how Carole met her former husband and what happened don't really fit here. She's nervous and has a lot invested in the outcome of this job interview. She wouldn't be letting her concentration wander by thinking about how she met her husband and why they didn't have kids, etc. She'd want to stay alert, in the present, ready for the next question.

If you want a character to reminisce about her past, make sure it's in a quiet scene where it would be natural, like if she's driving somewhere or waiting at the doctor's office. Also, keep the reminiscing brief so you don't stall out the story.

## ~ Author word choices and phrasing that aren't natural for the character.

If a blue-collar male character uses perfect grammar, complete sentences, and sophisticated words in casual dialogue or thoughts, that's the author who's not in tune with the character. Be sure your character's style of speaking and word choices reflect his education and social standing. If you want to wax poetic and show off your literary skills, you could always create a flamboyant, artistic type character who has a way with words.

# SOME EVEN MORE SUBTLE AUTHOR INTRUSIONS THAT CAN CREEP INTO YOUR STORY

## ~ Switching back and forth from the character's voice to the author's narration.

A more subtle form of author intrusion is when the voice and tone of the narration is markedly different from the words and thoughts of the viewpoint character, making the description and observations stand out as the author's voice, not the character's. This sets up a dichotomy and distances the readers from the character, when they want to *be* the character. Keep the narration in the same tone as the character's speech and natural thought patterns. That will give your whole novel a unique, authentic narrative voice, which isn't possible if your narration is more neutral and correct and "authorly."

So don't pull back and use a smooth, polished voice when describing the scene or another character, then go back to the short, clipped sentences of your down-to-earth male character. Make sure the whole scene, including the narration, is in your character's voice.

## ~ Author puts herself in the novel.

The author projects her own interests, likes, and dislikes onto her main character.

Many developing authors may be totally unaware that they're projecting their own preferences and knowledge base onto characters who likely wouldn't share their background or interests.

The solution to this is to create a detailed character profile, much of which will never make it into the story. Take the time to develop characters who are unique, multi-dimensional, and different from you.

To do this, try journaling in the characters' voices, using their words, phrasing, attitudes, and opinions. This will help you stay "in character" when writing the story, which will also give your story a strong, appealing, unique voice, which is so important.

**~ Author uses his fiction to pursue a personal agenda.**

It's all right to have your protagonist share some of your opinions and views, but try to be fair about it, and present opposing views as well. And don't make the opposition idiotic, unreasonable, or nasty just to weaken their credibility.

**~ Author inserts current or trendy words, terms, and expressions in stories taking place in foreign countries, especially disadvantaged or third-world countries.**

Be sure to stick with words that reflect that environment and situation.

## TECHNIQUES FOR AVOIDING OR FIXING AUTHOR INTRUSIONS

When writing fiction, remember that your primary goal is to entertain, so try to keep your personal agendas out of your stories. Any time the reader can spot the writer stepping in, whether it's blatant preaching, information dumping, or using words that would be foreign to the character, they'll be distracted, yanked out of the story world, and end up annoyed with the writer.

Remember, it's all about the story, and your characters need to have their own opinions, based on their background. Let them be themselves, be unique and quirky, with their own personality, views, and ways of expressing themselves.

**How to prevent or fix author intrusions in your own fiction.**

First, put the story aside for a few weeks or even a month or two to gain some distance from it and be able to view it more objectively, as a reader.

Do an editing pass where you're specifically looking for instances of any of the author intrusions mentioned above. Look for your biases, social views, pet topics, or buzzwords. Would that character really think or speak that way in those circumstances?

Ask beta (volunteer) readers or members of your critique group to be on the lookout for any anomalies, such as opinions that seem out of character, details the person probably wouldn't know, or words they probably wouldn't use.

## Questions to ask yourself

Here are some questions to guide your revisions:

~ Have I inadvertently given a character my own pet words, phrasing, and expressions? Would that character actually speak like that, given their background and personality?

~ Have I given my character knowledge and terminology that, given their age, education, station in life, and interests, they're unlikely to be familiar with? Watch for specialized terms such as names of trees, shrubs, flowers, and birds; names of bones; sports trivia; terminology associated with gourmet cooking or high fashion; historical or geographical details; and technological or mechanical specifics.

~ If I'm writing historical fiction or part of my story takes place in the past, have I taken care not to insert words and expressions that weren't in use in that era? This of course applies to dialogue, but even recently coined words inadvertently inserted into the narration of historical fiction can jolt the readers out of the story and erode the author's credibility.

~ For a novel set in in a different culture, such as in a remote area or third world, have I taken care not to insert words, expressions, customs, or worldviews used in affluent, educated urban or suburban America?

~ Do most of my characters speak differently from each other, or do most of them speak like me, the author? Do characters of the opposite sex speak differently?

~ Am I using character dialogue to educate readers on a topic? Does it sound natural to that character, rather than lecturing? Is there a better way to convey that information to the readers? Or do they even need that info?

~ When a character walks into a room or another character arrives, am I having my POV character notice details they wouldn't care about or be thinking about at that moment? Descriptions of the setting or other characters should only include details that character would actually note in that situation, given what else is going on.

As a fiction writer, your overarching goal should be to remain invisible as the author. Stay behind the scenes and let the reader follow the characters directly, as they want to, rather than butting in as a go-between to remind readers of key points, alert them to others, and tell them how to think and feel. Readers really hate that – they feel manipulated. They want to be left alone to react to events in the story world as they wish, to draw their own conclusions, to make the story their own. They want to forget their cares and be swept away by the story and characters.

Readers choose fiction for an engaging story and fascinating characters, to lose themselves in a world different and more exciting than their own. They don't choose fiction to learn about the author or find out the writer's opinions on topics.

So be careful not to break the magic spell of the story by reminding readers they're just reading a book by you, the author.

# Chapter 21 – A Strong Fictive Voice Needs Attitude

I attend a lot of writing conferences and read scores of craft-of-fiction books, and the topic of creating an appealing "voice" always comes up. Agents and aspiring editors are always looking for "a fresh voice," and aspiring (and even published) authors want to know how to develop an authentic, compelling voice that readers will love.

*The Reunion by John Cheever – Why not My Dad?*

To me, the best way is to **let the characters tell the story**. Stay out of the story as the author, and forget omniscient point of view.

Some examples of strong, unique voices that sweep us immediately into the character's world and the fictive dream are Huck's in *Huckleberry Finn*, Holden Caulfield's in *Catcher in the Rye*, Scout's in *To Kill a Mockingbird*, Stephanie Plum's in Janet Evanovich's series, and Katniss's in *The Hunger Games*.

These novels are all written in the first person, so of course it's a lot easier for the author to immerse us in the character's attitudes and worldview – especially with such fascinating characters.

But we can create an equally strong, appealing voice in third-person, too, if we take a tip from first-person POV and keep not only the dialogue, but the narration (observations and explanations) for each scene firmly in the character's viewpoint, using their words and colored by their background, personality, attitudes, and mood.

Also, try to have at least 70% of the novel in the protagonist's point of view, as he or she is the "star" of the story.

## Narration is the POV character's thoughts and observations

Does the narration of your novel sound like you, the author, talking to your readers? In other words, are your descriptions and explanations bland, neutral author intrusions? If so, you can draw your readers deeper into your character's psyche and your story world by making the narration, not just the dialogue, sound like the viewpoint character for that scene.

As your character moves through her environment, let the "camera" show only what she would be observing. Color the descriptions with her mood, attitude, and emotional and physical reactions. Make it her observations, not yours as the author. That will bring your character and story to life and make the voice for each scene sound more authentic.

In first-person novels, it's easy to create an authentic voice, as long as you've got a charismatic lead character. In stories written in third-person, strive to keep the internal monologue and narration in the main or POV character's voice. Let your viewpoint character's mood and attitudes and observations color your descriptions and explanations. That way your novel will come to life as a fascinating story world.

Don't fall into writing description and exposition as a nonfiction writer would. That's too distancing. You want the reader to remain immersed in your story world, in the fictive dream, so keep them up close and personal with your protagonist and other key characters. Stay in character for the narration too, not only the dialogue.

If you feel a point needs explaining to your readers, do it through your characters, not as an author intrusion. Make it a question-and-answer dialogue, with attitude and some tension. That keeps us right there, up close and personal, with your characters, not suddenly backed off to get a mini-lecture from the writer about a technical point or background info.

To grasp this concept and put it into practice in your work in process, think of it this way: Narration is really the character's thoughts. Each scene is told from a particular character's point of view, whether it's your protagonist (main character for the whole novel), a love interest, the antagonist/villain, or another important character. You're in that character's head and reacting as he/she is reacting. Extend that to the narration too.

Stay right in that character's viewpoint for as much of that scene as you can. This deep point of view draws the readers more deeply into your story and ensures that you're following that critical guideline for compelling fiction: *Show, don't tell*. If you're in your character's head and not butting in as the author to explain things to the readers, you're showing, not telling. Showing brings your story to life for the readers.

It's easiest to demonstrate this principle by using bad guys or rough-edged good guys or volatile, troubled characters or young children, as their voice is most distinctive, likely quite different than that of the author.

Here's an example of a skewed, dark description through the thoughts and observations of a nasty character, a murderer with no conscience, by talented writer Dara Carr, in her thriller, *The Overthrow*. The setting is a popular tourist attraction on the Pacific Coast, Cannon Beach, Oregon, with its much-photographed Haystack Rock:

> A gusty wind drove a spray of grit and salt at the van's pitted old windshield. He ran the wipers to clear his sightline. The condos, once white, looked shell-shocked and gray. In another year Marr figured the entire place would turn into driftwood.
>
> Expensive driftwood. The condos were beachfront property. Personally, he wouldn't pay a dime to live there. The Oregon coastline, jagged and sharp like the edge of a serrated knife, was good for one thing only: boat crashes.
>
> And the famous Haystack Rock? Plastered with bird shit. Home to Dr. Death, who'd plot the end of the world from his roost on top of the rock.

And the same scornful villain thinks about the story's two protagonists, female detectives:

> He glanced at his watch. Mom Langford and the lady detectives would be arriving soon. Not that the detectives worried him.
>
> One was as tall as a running back, with huge knockers and a rat's nest hairdo. Nails like daggers. She could carve bloody tracks down a man's back. He doubted she was good for much else. The other one, blond with black roots, looked a biscuit short of 160, with thighs like tree trunks and a swimmer's broad shoulders. She wore a permanent scowl, which he liked. Get her angry enough and she'd self-destruct.

For an authentic, engaging "voice" in third-person, stay in the POV character's head in the narration, too.

## TIPS FOR CREATING A STRONG THIRD-PERSON VOICE:

### ~ Start with a fascinating character readers will identify with and root for.

Your main character needs to be charismatic enough to carry the whole novel, so it's critical to take the time to first create a protagonist who's engaging and multi-dimensional, with lots of personality and openness, fairly strong views, and some vulnerability and inner conflict. Then be sure to show his world and the events unfolding around him through his eyes and ears, not the author's, or that of an omniscient narrator.

### ~ Write the narration from the character's point of view, too.

Stay in your character's POV for the observations, descriptions, and explanations, too, not just the dialogue and any inner thoughts and reactions. It's your character who's moving through that world, reacting to what's around him. Don't describe the surroundings and what's going on from a distant, neutral, authorial point of view –

show the character's world directly through her observations, colored by her personality and mood.

Here's one of many examples I could give from my editing of fiction, with details, setting, and circumstances altered for anonymity:

*Setup:* This is a flashback, a ten-year-old's frightened observations as, hidden behind a tree, she watches some bad guys in the woods.

*Before:*

> Suzie peered around the tree again to watch. The heavyset man pulled out a knife and strode toward the older, slimmer one. The slim man looked stunned, like he didn't expect that. In one swift movement, the tall man guy plunged the dagger into the older man's carotid artery. Bright red blood gushed out like a river.

We're in the point of view of a ten-year-old who is observing this and telling us what she sees. I doubt she'd know the term "carotid artery," much less exactly where it is. Also, she probably wouldn't say "heavyset man," "dagger," or "in one swift movement." And likely not "strode," either.

*After:*

> Suzie peered around the tree again to watch. The big man pulled out a knife and charged toward the older, slimmer one. The thin guy looked at him, his eyes wide. Before he could do anything, the big guy raised the knife and plunged it into his neck. Bright red blood gushed out like a river.

To me, this sounds more like a ten-year-old telling us this now, so we're staying in the voice of the POV character observing the scene.

Look through your any fiction projects you're working on. Does the narration (description and exposition) read like the main character for that scene could be thinking or saying it, or is it someone else's (the author's) words and phrasing? Are the descriptions of the surroundings neutral? Or are they colored and enriched by the character's feelings, goal, mood, and attitude at that moment?

**~ Let the characters do the explaining – in a spirited way.**

Even explanations of points should be presented through the characters, perhaps in a dialogue with disagreement and attitude.

Be on the lookout for where you step in as the author to blandly and dispassionately explain things to the readers, as if it's nonfiction. Besides being a less engaging read, that approach yanks us out of the character's mind-set and world – and out of the fictive dream.

## TOOLS FOR FINDING AND DEVELOPING THE POV CHARACTER'S VOICE:

Here are a few little techniques for livening up information-sharing and imparting it with attitude, from the viewpoint of the POV character involved.

**~ Use stream-of-consciousness journaling.**

To bring out the character's personality in the parts where he's thinking or planning or worrying or ruminating, not only when he's interacting with others, do some stream-of-consciousness journaling by him. Have him ranting in a personal diary about the people around him, what's going on, etc. Also show his deepest fears and his strongest desires or hopes here. Then use this wording to show his personality more in the scenes.

**~ Write the scene in first-person first, then switch it back.**

Write a whole scene, or even a chapter or two, in first-person narration/POV to get the rhythm and flow of that person's language patterns and attitudes, then rewrite it in third-person.

**~ Write a dialogue between you and the character**, with some disagreement and bantering or tension. That way you will see if you both sound the same or if your character has their own distinct voice.

## ~ Include lots of attitude and strong reactions.

To bring the scene and characters to life, write not only the dialogue and inner thoughts, but most of the narration in the POV of the main character for that scene, using their words and expressions, colored by their mood, with plenty of personality.

# Chapter 22 – Show the Setting through Your POV Character

One of the most effective ways to bring your story world and characters to life is to portray the surroundings through the senses, feelings, reactions, and attitude of your protagonist. Enhancing your fiction by filtering the description of the settings through the viewpoint character is a concept I instinctively embraced when I first started editing fiction years ago.

I was working on a contemporary middle-school novel in which the two main characters, a boy and a girl, were both eleven years old (I've changed the details slightly). The author had them describing rooms they entered as if they were interior decorators, complete with words like "exquisite," "stylish," "coordinated," "ornate," and "delightful." Then, when they were in the park or the woods playing and exploring with friends, each tree, shrub and flower was accurately named and described in details that were way beyond the average preteen's knowledge base or interests.

Besides the obvious problem of too much description for this target readership (or for any fiction today), this omniscient, literary, "grownup" way of describing their environment would not only turn off young readers due to the complex terms and sophisticated language, but also create a distance between any reader and these two modern-day kids.

As a reader and editor, I didn't feel like I was getting to know these kids at all, as I wasn't seeing their world through their eyes, but directly from the author, who obviously knew her interior design terms and flora and fauna! By separating us from the main characters through this unchildlike, out-of-character description of their environment, the author inadvertently puts a kind of semi-transparent wall between us and the two kids. If we don't get into their heads and hearts, seeing their world as they see it, how will we get to know them, and why will we care what happens to them?

So show us directly what the viewpoint character is seeing around him, in his own words and thoughts, colored by his attitude toward his surroundings. To bring the character and story to life on the page, evoke more senses than the visual. Tell us what he's hearing and smelling, too. And touching/feeling – the textures of things, and whether he's feeling warm or cold, wet or dry. Even the odd taste. And don't forget mood – how does that setting make him feel? Emotionally uplifted? Fearful? Warm and cozy? Include telling details specific to that place, and have the characters react to their environment, whether it's shivering from the cold, in awe of a gorgeous sunset, or afraid of the dark. Bring that scene to life through your characters' reactions.

Here's a great example of including sensory impressions, from *Nerve Damage*, a medical thriller by Tom Combs

> He entered the autopsy theater where Kip Dronen's gaunt body hunched over a stainless steel table. His surgical mask hung loose beneath over-sized wire-rim glasses and Einstein hair. The cloying odor of formaldehyde hung heavy. Underneath, Drake registered the sewer-air tinge of dead flesh.
>
> The brightly lit corpse of an elderly black male lay on the table. The standard Y-incision exposed the contents of the chest and abdomen. Kip wrestled a knobby softball-sized organ from the abdominal cavity. He plunked it into a basin dangling from a scale just above table height.
>
> "Son of a bitch, ER, sneak attack at dawn, huh?" squeaked Kip. He toed a foot pedal, turning off the microphone he used to record his findings. "See this?" He held his hands toward the body. "I'm under nut-crushing

pressure on your celebrity crump and I still have this bullshit to deal with."

As Donald Maass says in *Writing the Breakout Novel*, "Place presented from an objective or omniscient point of view runs the risk of feeling like boring descriptive. It can be a lump, an impediment to the flow of the narrative."

He continues, "Do you have plain vanilla description in your current manuscript? Try evoking the description the way it is experienced by a character. Feel a difference? So will your readers."

James Scott Bell also advises us, in *Revision & Self-Editing*, to "marble" the description of the environment in during the action. "The way to do this is to put the description in the character's point of view and use the details to add to the mood."

Jack M. Bickham gets more specific on this in *The 38 Most Common Fiction Writing Mistakes*: "When you start a scene in which Bob walks into a large room, for example, you do not imagine how the room looks from some god-like authorial stance high above the room, or as a television camera might see it; you see it only as Bob sees it, coming in…." And include what he's feeling, hearing, and smelling, too. Filter the scene through his perceptions and feelings. "This leads to reader identification with Bob, which is vital if the reader is to have a sense of focus."

**Don't describe scenes as the author – stay in the character's viewpoint.**

To have a strong narrative voice and a story that engages and enthralls readers, take care never to describe scenes or characters neutrally, like the author talking to the readers. Color all descriptions through the character who is observing what's going on.

Keep it authentic. What would that character actually notice at a moment like that?

For example, at times of stress, a character probably wouldn't be sightseeing or cataloguing the features of a room. He'd be concentrating on the source of stress and how to deal with the situation. In order to figure out how to handle a difficult person, your hero needs to study that person for clues, be watchful for any changes in mood, etc. For example, if he's being called on the carpet and in danger of being fired, it's unlikely he'd be idly looking around the room, noting various features of the decor.

To illustrate what I mean here, I've made up a scenario, loosely based on similar descriptions in stories I've edited. Our protagonist Travis is called in to meet the biggest boss, whom he's never met before. Travis knows he's in trouble and is worried about being fired.

*Before:*

> Travis straightened his tie and knocked lightly.
>
> "Enter."
>
> He opened the door and walked in.
>
> The boss's huge corner office overlooked Manhattan's skyline. Fluorescent tubes hummed overhead, the blue-green vapor tube glowing over Thompson's vast mahogany desk, a four-drawer filing cabinet, and a matching wood bookshelf filled with the volumes of the Laws of the State of New York. The desk held several files, neatly stacked. Edward Thompson, portly and in his sixties, studied a file in front of him, his reading glasses perched on his red nose. Travis stood there, then cleared his throat. Thompson looked up and glared at him from under bushy black eyebrows. Travis hoped his face was always that red, and not caused by fury.
>
> "Sit."
>
> "Yes, sir."

What's wrong with this detailed description of the boss's room here? When you walk into the office of a superior under stressful circumstances, it's highly unlikely you'd be noticing the fluorescent tubes and desk and cabinets and bookshelves, down to reading the spines of the books. The very first thing you look at is the person to gauge their mood, to try to ascertain how much trouble you're in. Upon entering the room, Travis would zero right in on the boss, so he needs to be described immediately.

*After:*

> Travis straightened his tie and knocked lightly.
>
> "Enter."
>
> He opened the door and walked in.
>
> Edward Thompson, portly and in his sixties, sat at his mahogany desk in his corner office overlooking the Manhattan skyline, a file open in front of him, his reading glasses perched on his red nose. Travis stood there, then cleared his throat. Thompson looked up and glared at him from under bushy black eyebrows. Travis hoped his face was always that red, and not caused by fury.
>
> "Sit."
>
> "Yes, sir."

Here's another example where the author has stepped in to describe a building, instead of staying in the viewpoint and voice of the character.

*Before:*

> Gonzales walked toward the entrance of the large weather-beaten building nestled among a grove of pomegranate trees. Inside the building, the laboratory consisted of multiple tables with equipment and chemicals used in transforming the sticky milk-colored poppy gum into heroin. He felt totally at home inside this building, since it's where he had spent most of his life.

In the passage above, we're in Gonzales' point of view, but the description of the facility, which he is very familiar with, is as if the author is stepping in to tell us about it. It's more organic and natural

137

to stay in Gonzales' head instead of jumping to omniscient point of view just to describe the laboratory.

*After:*

> Gonzales strode through the grove of pomegranate trees toward the entrance of the large weather-beaten building. Inside, he strolled through the family-owned laboratory, talking with workers and inspecting the equipment and chemicals they used to transform the sticky milk-colored poppy gum into heroin. His father had built this heroin lab and Gonzales had grown up here, so as the young *jefe*, he commanded respect.

As always, there are so many ways to rewrite the passage, and this is only one possibility.

# Chapter 23 – Sensory Details Suck Your Readers In

How often do you hear – or feel – about a rejected novel, "I just couldn't get into it"? A story might have a great premise and plot, but if we don't find ourselves drawn quickly into the story world, we'll probably put it down and look for another one.

What are some aspects of a novel that make you yawn, go "meh," or start thinking about what else you could be doing? I would bet that most times it's because the author hasn't succeeded in engaging you emotionally, in effectively sucking you into their story world, making you feel like you're right there with the characters.

After a long day of editing, when it comes to evening reading, I'm going for entertainment and escapism. I want to lose myself in a novel, not be a detached observer of the characters and events. Don't you?

In my editing of fiction, I sometimes see too much general, factual exposition ("info dumps") or neutral, mostly visual description. Or there's a page or more of straight dialogue ("talking heads"), with little or no indication of where the characters are, what they're doing, what they're seeing, hearing, smelling, touching, or tasting, or how they're feeling/reacting to others and their environment.

> "Good writing is supposed to evoke sensation in the reader – not the fact that it is raining, but the feeling of being rained upon."
>
> ~ E. L. Doctorow

In order for your story and characters to come to life on the page, your readers need to be able *see* what the main character is seeing, *hear* what he's hearing, and *smell, taste* and *feel* what he does.

And to empathize with and bond with the character, readers also need to see/feel his reactions and thoughts.

> "If you write abstractions or judgements, you are writing an essay, whereas if you let us use our senses and form our own interpretations, we will be involved as participants in a real way."
>
> ~ Janet Burroway, *Writing Fiction*

So if you've written a half-page or more of nonstop dialogue, neutral information-sharing, or description that's mainly visual, it's time for some revisions.

To bring your scene and characters to life and engage the readers, evoke all or most of the five senses in almost every scene.

## SIGHT

Readers need to see what your viewpoint character sees: pertinent visual impressions of the scene and people around him. And best to include only relevant information, the things that character would actually notice in that scene. We don't need a detailed description of everything in a room, for example – they're usually too busy acting and reacting to study the room thoroughly.

Zoom in on some telling details, like smudges on a mirror, sweat on a brow, condensation on a glass, steam from a coffee cup, fists clenched, hands shaking, shoulders hunched, etc.

A small sampling of visual descriptors:

glaring, faded, dim, bright, dingy, flashing, dazzling, blurred, sparkling, brilliant, flashy, radiant, shadowy, smudged, streaked, glistening, shiny, gaudy, gleaming, glittering, gloomy, glowing, hazy, misty, shimmering, streaked, twinkling, tarnished.

Here are a few examples of evocative visual description in some classic novels:

"...people on the bridges peeping over the parapets into a nether sky of fog, with fog all round them, as if they were up in a balloon, and hanging in the misty clouds."

~ *Bleak House*, by Charles Dickens

"vivid flashes of lightning dazzled my eyes, illuminating the lake, making it appear like a vast sheet of fire; then for an instant everything seemed of a pitchy darkness...

"... I perceived in the gloom a figure... A flash of lightning illuminated the object, and discovered its shape plainly to me; its gigantic stature, and the deformity of its aspect, more hideous than belongs to humanity, instantly informed me that it was the wretch, the filthy daemon..."

~ *Frankenstein*, by Mary Shelley

**SOUNDS**

We need to hear anything your POV character can perceive, including tone of voice.

Some sound verbs:

swish, rattle, crash, whack, crackle, gulp, slam, hoot, clatter, crunch, fizz, grind, gurgle, blare, chime, slap, chirp, chortle, thud, chuckle, clash, croak, rumble, croon, drone, groan, howl, jangle, knock, ping, jingle, plop, roar, rustle, sizzle, slurp, thunk, tinkle, twang, whine, whistle.

Example of sounds:

"...the storm came rattling over the Heights in full fury. ... a huge bough fell across the roof, and knocked down a portion of the east chimney-stack, sending a clatter of stones and soot into the kitchen-fire."

~ *Wuthering Heights*, by Emily Bronte

## SCENTS

Include anything that might be pertinent or bring the scene to life – fresh coffee, an apple pie baking, bacon frying, a suspicious chemical smell, fresh-cut grass, the stench of a dead body decomposing, etc.

Some possible descriptors for scent:

musty, damp, stuffy, sweet, sickly, rank, spicy, acidic, perfumed, fetid, musky, suffocating, putrid, tantalizing, mouth-watering, noxious, sharp, foul, rancid, stinky, funky, pungent, piney.

Example of smells:

> "…they were crammed in a tiny apartment that smelled of burning rubber and foot odor."
>
> ~ *Holes*, by Louis Sachar

## TOUCH

We should feel any relevant tactile sensations of the viewpoint character.

Some tactile sensations to consider:

sticky, fuzzy, slimy, clammy, hairy, silky, smooth, rough, soft, hard, rigid, fluffy, starchy, crisp, corrugated, rippled, abrasive, cracked, tough, bristly, burning, cold, cottony, damp, dry, feathery, furry, gnarled, hot, knobbed, knotted, leathery, limp, lumpy, oily, puffy, ribbed, rubbery, sandy, sharp, smooth, velvety, wet.

Example of touch:

> "On every rail and gate, wet lay clammy."
>
> ~ *Great Expectations*, by Charles Dickens

# TASTE

Let us vicariously taste some of the things the character is eating or drinking.

Some descriptors for tastes:

sour, bitter, oily, salty, acidic, spicy, fiery, sweet, rich, buttery, sugary, revolting, biting, fruity, full-bodied, gamy, gross, juicy, sharp, succulent, syrupy, tangy, tart, zesty, zingy.

Example of taste:

"Slimy water that tasted like blenderized fishsticks slid down my throat."

~ *Crown Me!* by Kathryn Lay

**Bring the scene alive by evoking as many of the senses as possible.**

Which of these two scenes makes you feel as if you are right there with this boy, lost in the woods?

Before:

Kevin trudged through the forest, listening for sounds. How had he let himself get separated from the group? He heard rushing water and headed toward it.

After:

Wet and cold, Kevin trudged through the Pacific Northwest rainforest, listening for sounds of his friends. Fighting back panic, he tried to ignore the painful blisters on his feet from the chafing of his new hiking books. After tromping around for hours, crunching over dead leaves, pushing aside undergrowth, and tripping over tree roots, his muscles felt like jelly and his legs threatened to buckle under him. How had he let himself get separated from the group? His shirt was still damp from the spill in the creek and a cool breeze made him shiver. He really wished he'd worn a jacket.

Now and then he paused to sniff the air, hoping to catch a whiff of smoke from the campfire, but all he smelled was the damp moss, stinky skunk cabbage, and fragrant cedar trees. The lengthening shadows and the caws and rustles and strange animal sounds made his stomach tighten in fear. In the distance he heard rushing water. He hiked toward it and ended up at another burbling stream. Or was it the one he fell into earlier? Had he been walking in circles? Everything looked the same. *Crap.* He kneeled and used his hands to scoop up some of the cool, clear water to drink, exhausted and numb. If he stayed here, at least he had fresh water – and that one granola bar. Should he eat it now? If he survived the night in the wild, maybe they'd find him tomorrow. *Don't panic. They'll find you.*

Here's an excerpt from a published thriller, where a mother and her two children have been kidnapped and are bound and gagged in a remote location. She's found a gas stove and is determined to burn off the constraints binding her wrists behind her back. With the use of smells, sounds, the visual, her pain, her muscles quivering, the scene is vivid and convincing.

> Closing her eyes, she lowered her wrists.
>
> She gasped, then gave a prolonged gag-muffled scream. The stink of burnt hair, the pops and crackles of incinerating clotted blood, and pain rocketing beyond her imagination.
>
> She held her children in her mind's eye as she sacrificed her flesh to the fire. Torture without limit. Her face twisted and pulled. The smell of charring flesh, her muscles quivering, then involuntarily bucking as she willed herself to endure. Colors flashed in her head, her wrists a blacksmith's forge.

She strained at the restraint with all she had. Her vision raced to black and her moan expired.

She pitched forward to the floor.

~ *Nerve Damage*, by Tom Combs

So if you want to write riveting fiction (and who doesn't?), don't keep your readers at a distance, impassively reading the words on the page. Suck them right into your story world, your fictive dream, by making them feel like they're right there with your character, like they are your character. Evoke sights, sounds, smells, and tastes from the readers' own memory banks, which will trigger emotions. Scents especially bring back feelings and memories that readers can draw upon to be active participants in your story.

And show us what the characters are thinking and feeling, too – their inner and outer reactions to what's going on around them. All of this enhances the readers' experience and deepens their emotional investment with your story.

# Chapter 24 – Show Character Reactions to Bring Them to Life

## CONTINUALLY REVEAL YOUR CHARACTERS' FEELINGS & REACTIONS

A novel won't draw me in unless I start caring about the protagonist and worrying about what's going to happen to him – in other words, until I get emotionally engaged in the story. For me to warm up to the protagonist, he has to have some warmth and vulnerability and determination, some hopes and insecurities and fears. If he doesn't care, if he's not moved or angered or shocked or afraid or delighted, why should I be? And it's the same for most readers, I think.

As readers, to identify with and bond with the protagonist, we need to see and feel their emotions and reactions to people and events around them. When the character feels and reacts, they come alive for us, and we get emotionally invested and start to worry about them and cheer for their small victories. Once you have your readers fretting about your heroine and rooting for her, they're hooked.

Even if you're writing a thriller or action-adventure, emotional reactions are always more powerful than just having your character observing or considering something. Never hesitate to show how your characters are feeling about things. As the late, great Jack M. Bickham said in *The 38 Most Common Fiction Writing Mistakes*, "Fiction characters who only think are dead. It is in their feelings that the readers will understand them, sympathize with them, and care about their plight."

In my editing of fiction I quite often make comments like, "This is significant. Show his reaction to this." or "How is she feeling about this?"

For example, in one book I edited, a young rookie is watching an autopsy for the very first time. The author describes in graphic detail the incisions, pulling out organs, etc., with no reactions whatsoever from this observer, whose head and body we're in. I imagine someone who's never witnessed an autopsy would be feeling a bit (or a lot) nauseated, and the smell would be getting to her – not to mention feelings of repulsion, or at least fascination. We're in this rookie's point of view so to bring the situation to life, we need to experience the autopsy from inside her head and body and feel her physical and emotional reactions.

**Show those feelings.**

So bring your characters to life by showing their deepest fears, worries, frustrations, hopes, and jubilations. If readers see your hero pumped, scared, angry, shocked, or worried, they'll feel that way, too. And a reader who is feeling strong emotions is a reader who is turning the pages.

**And sensations.**

Engage the readers' senses, too, so they feel like they're right there, by showing us not only what the character is seeing, but what they're hearing, smelling, touching, sensing, and even tasting.

**Show their physical reactions, too.**

Besides showing us your character's emotional reactions, show her physical reactions as well to what's happening to her. And have her react immediately to what's just occurred, as we do in real life. And since we're in her head and body, don't show her reaction before we know what she saw or heard or touched – in other words, what she's reacting to.

147

**Show the stimulus before the response, and show the reactions in their natural order.**

To avoid reader confusion and annoyance, be sure to state the cause before the effect, the stimulus before the response, the action before the reaction. In other words, show character reactions immediately and in the order they occur. *(intuitive, instinct, emotional)*
*(rather than intellectual)*
To mirror reality, it's important to **show your character's visceral reaction to a situation first**, before an overt action or words. And show involuntary thought-reactions or word-reactions, like a quick "ouch" or swear word, before more reasoned thought processes and decision-making.

In this "before" example, the POV character is reacting too calmly to suddenly having a gun pointed at her. Even if she doesn't want to respond outwardly, she should be reacting more inwardly.

*Before:*

> "You think my son did it?" He reached into his pocket, pulled out a gun, and pointed it at me.
> Not the reaction I had expected.
> "Whoa," I said, putting my hands up, as if they would stop a bullet. "I'm not accusing anybody of anything."

We need to see both the accuser's outward reactions and the narrator's stress at being threatened with a gun.

*After:*

> "You think my son did it?" He reached into his pocket, pulled out a gun, and pointed it at me, his face flushed, his eyes narrowed.
> My heart started pounding and my mouth suddenly went dry. I could hear my blood rushing.
> "Whoa," I said, putting my hands up, as if they would stop a bullet. "I'm not accusing anybody of anything."

In this next example, our protagonist is locked in a basement and the rest of the house is on fire. In the first example, he's about to die and isn't reacting at all to this very real possibility.

*Before:*

> He looked around the basement. Concrete floor. Junk littered everywhere. In the corner stood three red plastic jugs, with handles and spouts. He went over and sniffed. Gasoline.
>
> He heard the wail of sirens getting closer. Sheila must have called them from her cell phone. As the sparks from the fire danced on the wood around him, he knew he couldn't wait for the fire trucks to arrive. He had to get out now.

*After:*

> He looked around the basement. Concrete floor. Junk littered everywhere. In the corner stood three red plastic jugs, with handles and spouts. He went over and sniffed. Gasoline.
>
> *Oh Lord. This is it. I'm going to die.* His skin went clammy and his head pounded as he thought about his wife and three kids. They need me. It's not fair. I'm too young to die.
>
> He heard the wail of sirens getting closer. Sheila must have called them from her cell phone. As the sparks from the fire danced on the wood around him, he knew he couldn't wait for the fire trucks to arrive. He had to get out now.

(As with all my examples, there are of course lots of different ways to improve the "before" passage, and you might come up with some even better ideas.)

## Show immediate thought-reactions.

In this disguised example from my editing, we're in police detective Jerome's POV.

*Before:*

> Chief Martin Swift walked into the room, followed closely by Mayor Roy Morrison. The expression on Morrison and Swift's faces indicated bad news was coming.
> "We need to meet, now," Chief Swift said.

*After:*

> Chief Martin Swift walked into the room, followed closely by Mayor Roy Morrison.
> *What the hell is Morrison doing here?* Jerome thought.
> "We need to meet, now," Chief Swift said.

Or leave out "Jerome thought," as the italics indicate a direct thought.

Here's another example of an immediate thought-reaction:

*Before:*

> Her phone vibrated. That must be him again. She'd missed his last call. She grabbed her coat and rushed toward the theater exit. Outside, she answered. Just a ringtone. The screen showed Ken again. She tried to call him back but got a busy signal.

She has been waiting for this call and has missed it again. We need to feel her frustration.

*After:*

> Her phone vibrated. That must be him again. She'd missed his last call. She grabbed her coat and rushed toward the theater exit. Outside, she answered. Just a ringtone. *Damn.* The screen showed Ken again. She tried to call him back

150

but got a busy signal. She ran her fingers through her hair. What's going on? Why is he calling?

In the "after" example, her thought-reactions and actions emphasize the importance of the call to her.

**Show the reactions of other characters, too.**

Show us how other characters are feeling and reacting by what the viewpoint character is observing – their words, actions, body language, facial expressions, and tone of voice. In this example, Morris is a police detective, and Bryson is a potential witness to a crime:

*Before:*

> "I'll need a taped statement from you, Bryson," Morris said.
> Bryson made a weak protest and said, "I don't know what good it'll do, since I already told you I had just left."
> "Just get it to me, ASAP."
> "Sure thing, Detective Morris," Bryson answered and then left.

Rather than "made a weak protest," it would be more effective to show this with gestures or words or facial expressions or body language. Then show Bryson's feelings or reactions before he leaves. Never miss a chance to increase tension by showing attitude and reactions.

*After:*

> "I'll need a taped statement from you, Bryson," Morris said.
> Bryson stiffened and folded his arms in front of him. "I don't know what good it'll do, since I already told you I had just left."
> "Just get it to me, ASAP."

"Sure thing, Detective Morris." Bryson's voice was syrupy. He glared at Mike, then turned and strode out.

Also, **show us your character's motivations** – make the connection for the readers between the character's desires and intentions and their actions to try to achieve those goals.

So be sure to enrich your characters and your scenes by showing us your POV character's reactions, feelings, and motivations.

**But don't be melodramatic.** Be careful not to go overboard with it – you don't want your protagonist to come across as gushing or hysterical or neurotic. It's important to strike a balance so the readers can relate to and empathize with your lead, not feel annoyed or disgusted with her and quit reading.

But how do we strike that balance? How do we as writers find the emotions to bring our characters to life, but also find a happy medium between flat, emotionless characters that bore us and hysterical drama queens or raging bulls that make us cringe?

Jack M. Bickham advises us to consider how we've felt in similar circumstances, then overwrite first, and revise down later. "I would much prefer to see you write too much of feeling in your first draft; you can always tone it down a bit later... On the other hand, a sterile, chill, emotionless story, filled with robot people, will never be accepted by any reader."

## SHOW CHARACTER REACTIONS IN THE ORDER THEY OCCUR

To make us feel what the character is feeling, indicate their reactions in the same order we experience them in real life. Here's a guideline for showing character reactions to stressful situations

**Show first whatever happens fastest, and show it immediately.** Remember, we're inside your heroine's head and body, so you deepen her character and draw us closer to her by showing us what she's feeling immediately inside – those involuntary physical and

152

thought reactions that come before controlled, civilized outward reactions.

**Show the stimulus before the response.** Show the action before the reaction, the cause before the effect.

**Show the reactions in the order they occur.** You may not indicate all of these reactions, but whichever ones you choose, describe them in this order: *intuitive, instinctive, emotional*

1. **The character's visceral response** — adrenaline surging, pulse racing, stomach clenching, heart pounding, mouth drying, flushing, shivering, cold skin, tense muscles, sweating, blushing, shakiness, etc.

2. **His unconscious knee-jerk physical action** – yelling, gasping, crying out, snatching hand or foot away from source of heat or pain, striking out, etc.

3. **His thought processes and decision to act**

4. **His conscious action or verbal response**

Showing your character's feelings and responses will bring him to life on the page for the readers and suck readers deeper into your story world, your fictive dream.

*intuitive, emotional*
**So start with her visceral reaction.** That's the involuntary physical reaction we have no control over, that happens despite all our best efforts to suppress it or hide it. These reactions occur immediately, before any thought processes or deliberate actions, so it's important to show your character's visceral reaction first. This mirrors reality and puts your readers inside the character's skin, feeling the fear or embarrassment or shock or anger right along with them. *Clara smiled to see Henry @ her door.*

**Next, show an immediate thought-reaction**, like *Ow!* or *Oh no!* or *Damn.* or *Omigod.* or *Idiot!* or *That can't be!* And note that these sudden, short thought-reactions are usually italicized, both for emphasis and immediacy, and to indicate a direct thought. Then go

153

on to show the characters' other, slightly delayed reactions, such as their words, actions, facial expressions, and body language.

But it's important to show those involuntary visceral reactions first. Psychotherapist Margie Lawson lists some **common visceral reactions to stressful actions, words or events:**

- stomach clenching
- heart pounding
- rapid and shallow breathing
- pulse racing
- adrenaline surging
- legs weakening
- throat tightening
- mouth drying
- face flushing
- nausea imminent
- chest tightening
- equilibrium failing
- hear blood rushing
- vision narrowing

As Lawson explains, "Visceral responses are involuntary. You can't keep your face from flushing. You can't keep your mouth from going dry. You can't keep your chest from tightening, your heart from pounding, your vision from narrowing. ... Visceral responses are experienced first. Always."

So when there's a strong emotional stimulus, people don't act first, think first, or speak first. They experience an involuntary response first. This is something they can't control.

**Be sure to show characters' reactions in the order that they naturally occur, and don't skip that important initial physical reaction.** Readers will recognize those reactions they themselves have felt, so they'll feel more deeply what the character is feeling and become more emotionally engaged with the character and their situation – your story.

But try to avoid overused, clichéd responses, which no longer have the power they once had. Similarly, don't keep using the same reactions over and over, or pile on too many visceral responses at once. Pick the best one or two for the situation, and save the rest for other scenes.

And to find just the right emotional, physical, or internal character reactions for any given situation or emotion, such as shock, embarrassment, anger, joy, fear, and worry, I highly recommend *The Emotion Thesaurus: A Writer's Guide to Character Expression,* by Angela Ackerman and Becca Puglisi.

*Margie Lawson, a psychotherapist, editor, and international presenter, teaches writers how to edit for psychological power, how to hook the reader viscerally, how to create a page-turner.*

# PART VI

# SPARK UP YOUR STYLE AND ADD TENSION & INTRIGUE

# Chapter 25 – Does Every Word Enhance the Tone and Mood of the Scene?

Is it possible you may have inadvertently inserted the odd "cheery" word into a tense scene in your story? Or a relaxed-sounding word in a scene where the character is in a hurry? I see this quite often in the fiction I edit. For example, the heroine and hero are running through the woods, pursued by bad guys intent on killing them. The author, thinking it's a good idea to describe the setting, uses words like "leaves dancing in the light" and "birds chirping" and "babbling brook." These light-hearted, cheerful words detract from the desperation she's trying to convey as the protagonists race for their survival. In this situation, it would be better to use more ominous words, perhaps crows cawing, a wolf howling, water crashing over rapids, or thunder cracking. Create location + atmosphere to suit theme, characters + action. description, dialogue

Read through each of your scenes and make sure every word you use to describe the setting, the people, and their actions, words, and thoughts enhances the mood and tone you're going for in that scene, rather than detracting from it. Creating atmosphere

Here's an example, slightly disguised, from my editing. It's supposed to be a tense, scary moment, but the author has inadvertently inserted relaxed, even joyful imagery that counteracts and weakens the apprehensive mood he is trying to convey (my bolding).

> He locked the door behind him, his harried mind ricocheting between frightened alertness and sheer fatigue. He took a furtive glance out the window. No one there, so far. Despite the cold, **a warming shaft of morning**

**sunlight** filtered through the stained curtain, and **languid dust particles slow-danced in its beam.**

What had he gotten himself into? They would certainly be on to him now—it was only a matter of time before they found him. He looked out again through the thin curtain. **Sunbeams** were filtering through the branches of an old tree outside the window, the shriveled shapes of the leaves **dancing in the breeze, playing gleefully with the light.** He swore he saw movement on the ground outside— a figure.

Some of the wording in the two paragraphs above is excellent, like "his harried mind ricocheting between frightened alertness and sheer fatigue" and the phrases "furtive glance," "stained curtain" and "shriveled shapes of the leaves." But the boldfaced words and phrases, *warming, languid, slow-danced, sunbeams, dancing in the breeze,* and *playing gleefully with the light* weaken the imagery and tone because they're too happy and carefree for the intended ominous mood. Perhaps the writer, caught up in describing the view outside in a literary, "writerly" way, momentarily forgot he was going for frightened.

Be sure your imagery all fits the overall mood and tone of the situation.

Here's another example where the description of the setting detracts from the power of the scene and doesn't match how the character would or should be feeling at that moment.

The protagonist has just had a shock at the end of the last chapter, where she's discovered her colleague murdered. This is the beginning of the next chapter, a jump of a few days.

Mary gazed at the **brightening horizon**, immersing herself in the **beauty of the rising sun**. She watched as the dawn's rays danced across the waves. Mary **adored this time of day** when the hustle and bustle had not yet started, and she could **enjoy watching the waves wash in and**

**listening to the seagulls overhead.** It was one of the many reasons **she loved this area so much.**

Since the murder of Teresa three days ago, Mary had been in a state of turmoil. Teresa's death had changed everything. Gruesome images continually flickered through her mind like an unending motion picture. She could think of nothing else and was racked by guilt.

To me, the two paragraphs seem contradictory in mood. If she's racked by guilt and can think of nothing else, how can she enjoy the sunrise so much?

**Use words that fit the mood you're trying to convey.**

Here's another example of a tense scene whose power and tension have been inadvertently eroded by almost comical imagery.

*Before:*

The room went black and shots rang out in the darkness.

He took to the floor on all fours and, panicking, **scrabbled around aimlessly,** searching his **addled mind** for a direction, a goal. He poked his head up and looked around. Spotted the red exit sign of the back door. **Loping ape-like** across the office floor, he tried to keep his body below the level of the desks—**he had seen them do it in the movies, so it was good enough for him.**

Several more bullets whistled overhead.

The words "addled" and "loping ape-like" seem too light and humorous for the life-or-death scene. Even the bit about seeing it in the movies, so it was good enough for him seems too light-hearted – this could be the last moments of this guy's life if he doesn't find a way to avoid the bullets!

Here's the same scene, rewritten to capture the desperate mood:

The room went black and shots rang out in the darkness.

*What the—?* He dropped to the floor and, panicking, searching his frenzied mind for a direction, a goal. *Get out of here!* He poked his head up and looked around. Spotted the red exit sign of the back door. At a low crouch, he set out across the open office, dodging from one desk to another.

Several more bullets whistled overhead.

Here's another example with imagery that's fresh and creative, but does it actually fit the moment?

A truck came barreling toward them. He wrenched the wheel to the right, and they passed the truck, missing it by inches. Mud splattered onto the windshield, and the wipers smeared it like **chocolate ice cream**.

I think the chocolate ice cream imagery, although clever, is too positive and playful for the tense, scary moment.

**The character's body language and actions should also match the situation.**

Don't have someone "strolling" when they're worried. Have them "pacing" instead. Similarly, when they're arguing, don't have them leaning back in their chair – have them hunched forward, or pointing a finger.

Here's a sentence involving a description of actions that don't seem to fit:

He stared at the threatening letter, massaging the tension from the back of his neck **with nimble fingers**, kneading it like dough.

The word "nimble" has a light, lively, cheery connotation that doesn't work here.

160

**Make sure every single word fits the scene and enhances the mood.**

Even one incompatible word can jolt the reader or dilute the power of a scene.

Can you pick out the word below that deflates the moment?

> The guard drew in a shuddering breath as if to cry out. He half-coughed and half-gasped, then started to scream again, this time with enthusiasm. Brad covered the man's mouth and knocked his gun to the ground.

Rather than screaming "with enthusiasm," I'd use "in desperation" or "in terror" or something like that. The choice of "with enthusiasm" evokes positive, cheery connotations.

Here's another example of just one word jolting us out of the mood:

> They broke the lock on the warehouse and looked around. "Let's check the big freezers in the back."
>
> He strode over and opened the freezer door. The smell of frozen flesh and blood smacked him in the face. An emaciated, naked man stared at him with lifeless eyes, frozen like a popsicle.

Yes, it's that word at the end. I imagine the writer was searching for a good word for "frozen like" but "popsicle" is an unfortunate choice as it evokes an image that's way too upbeat for the situation. Best to look for a more somber or horrific simile (maybe "like a pale slab of beef").

Read these short passages and see if you can pick out the single word in each that contradicts the desired mood and tone.

1. As the realization of what had happened hit her, Linda gasped and dropped to her knees, a myriad of twirling thoughts bombarding her mind.

2. Could Greg have sold him out, led him here into a trap? Tony fixed his friend with an intense stare brimming with disappointment and betrayal.

161

3. In the interrogation room, the accused man's stiff, jaunty movements, drumming fingers, and constant glances around made Derek wonder if he was on something.

4. "We've never met but you know me," the stranger said. His hoarse voice reflected a coldness which Susan could only imagine as coming from evil.

5. He ran out of the burning building and stumbled away from the gaggle of press. He limped along, breathing deeply, trying to clear his head.

6. The car spun on an invisible axis then crashed into a light post. Steve's head bounced off the window, and his headache blossomed anew.


Words that don't fit:

1. "twirling" seems too light-hearted in this situation, like someone dancing or a baton twirling. Maybe "whirling" or "swirling."

2. "brimming" is too cheery, too positive. Maybe just "his voice filled with disappointment..."

3. "jaunty" seems too lighthearted here – too sprightly, lively. Maybe "erratic" or "awkward" or "nervous"?

4. "hoarse" is not bad, but it could be from a sore throat or cold, or even nervousness. I'd use "steely voice" or "rough" or "harsh."

5. "gaggle" seems too lighthearted, almost comical for the situation. I'd use "throng of press" or something similar.

6. "blossomed" is too positive for a headache caused by a crack on the head during a car accident.

# Chapter 26 – Avoid Overwriting – Subtle is More Sophisticated

Overwriting or over-the-top writing, where it's obvious the writer is trying way too hard to impress, can give an impression of lack of self-confidence and can scream "amateur" to industry professionals and discerning readers.

Many literary agents and acquiring editors cite overwriting as one of the most obvious errors in aspiring fiction writers (along with fuzzy point of view, boring openings, and stilted dialogue). As Anthony Brown and Darrin English say in *Stickman Review*, "Young writers, full of energy, throw everything and the kitchen sink into their work to impress editors."

The novice writer prone to overwriting will typically take a basic idea, image, or action and, rather than leaving it alone, will feel the need to expand on it. He'll keep adding more fancy descriptive words, mainly adjectives and adverbs, until the bloated passage has grown way out of proportion to its importance to the story as a whole. This kind of overkill stands out, and not in a good way, like someone with perfectly coiffed hair and heavy makeup wearing a glittery strapless gown, spike heels, and ornate jewelry to a casual backyard barbeque. Or like an overly decorated room, where the real treasures become lost among all the other ostentatious accessories and collectibles.

Overwriting can come across as showing off and can be a big turn-off. It can also be irritating, as all that extra flashy bling-bling gets in the way of the story we are trying to read. Readers start skimming to get back to the character and their intriguing, worrisome journey.

Also, new writers sometimes mistakenly think that good writing has to be elaborate. They haven't yet learned the power of simple, direct language and the value of "less is more." They're still gaining confidence and the courage to trim down passages they've labored over – and even, if necessary, to "kill their darlings."

Newbie writers may get enamored with the beauty of their prose and forget that it's not about them and their literary prowess – it's about the story, and the reader's entertainment and enjoyment. Sometimes that pleasure comes from a well-turned phrase or a well-chosen word, but the savvy writers will make sure they don't get carried away and stuff every scene to bloating.

Developing writers also aren't used to being edited or paring down their own work. They may feel that every word is sacred because they've labored over it. But it takes experience to be able to see your writing from the viewpoint of agents, editors, and readers, and start deleting any overblown, overly lyrical passages to cut to the core.

**What exactly is overwriting?**

What are some of the signs that signal a forced effort and lack of confidence on the part of the writer? Here's what three writers have to say on the subject:

Writing guru Richard Nordquist defines overwriting as "a wordy writing style characterized by excessive detail, needless repetition, overwrought figures of speech, and/or convoluted sentence structures."

Author and craft writer Paula LaRocque says, "Overwriting is the failure to make choices. .. Linguistic bric-a-brac is literature's Elvis on velvet."

Mary Kole describes this type of writer as "a scribe who uses $10 words and milks every image and otherwise packs every sentence

164

until it's dragging and bloated. They want to make sure we *get* they're a *real writer*." ("Two Signs of Overwriting and Why It's a Problem")

Overwriting, in its extreme, is also described as *flowery writing* or *purple prose*. According to the Oxford English Dictionary, purple prose is writing that is "too elaborate or ornate."

**Some signs of overwriting include:**

- too much description
- too many extravagant words
- too many adjectives and adverbs
- extreme reactions and over-the-top emotions
- too much detailed introspection,
- wordiness in general (bloated sentences and paragraphs)
- unnecessary repetition of words and concepts
- telling after you've shown

Another example is including a favorite scene or passage because you slaved over it and think it's lyrical or literary and will impress readers, but it doesn't really fit the story. Or it might have worked before but doesn't anymore, due to other changes you've made.

**Why is overwriting a problem?**

Not only can overwriting seem saccharine sweet or oily rich, but any of the above tendencies often stop the action, slow down pacing, and interrupt the forward flow of the story.

As Strunk and White say in *The Elements of Style*, "Rich, ornate prose is hard to digest, generally unwholesome, and sometimes nauseating."

Also, using too many words to get a message across gets in the way of quick comprehension and can be mind-numbing and annoying. As Durant Imboden puts it so succinctly, "Padded prose makes readers doze." You risk having readers skip those parts, and if it continues, they may decide to skip the rest of the book and find a better one.

Readers want to get immersed in a great story, and overwriting detracts from their experience and can be irritating enough to invite negative reviews.

**How do we recognize and correct the problem of overwriting in our manuscripts?**

As mentioned above, overwriting can be an exaggerated passage or scene. It can also be a cluttered paragraph or even an overly wordy sentence where fewer direct, to-the-point words would be much more succinct. Weeding is especially important in mundane scenes, where every little detail won't be of interest to most readers.

Fortunately, unlike a serious plot problem or lackluster characters, overwriting can be reined in through some judicious cutting and revisions. And as you get used to editing your own work, you'll gradually stop overwriting. It's all about paring down any overdone passages until you're left with only the words your story needs for the optimal impact, imagery, and tone you're after.

**Examples of overwriting:**

Here are a couple of overblown sentences depicting an ordinary scene that cries out for a good decluttering:

> She put the kettle on to boil, opened the cupboard, scanned her varieties of teas, chose a box of Earl Grey, pulled out a teabag, dropped it in the teapot, and added the boiling water. While it steeped, she took a fresh-baked carrot cake out of the refrigerator, sliced it, and arranged some pieces on a fancy plate.

Boiled down to its essence, it becomes something like:

> She made a pot of Earl Grey tea and served that with fresh-baked carrot cake.

All that extra detail in the first version is really not necessary; in fact, it slows down the pacing and can be quite boring to most readers. Often, less is more.

Here's a shorter sentence that contains extraneous words with mundane details that are cluttering it up:

He grabbed his coat, put it on, opened the door, went out, shut it behind him, descended the steps, and headed to his car, parked in the driveway.

Pared down, it becomes:

He grabbed his coat, went out, and headed to his car, parked in the driveway.

Or just:

He grabbed his coat and headed out to his car.

Sometimes a reflective scene calls for a more leisurely pace and more elaborate phrasing, but keep these more detailed passages to a minimum or you risk turning off your reader, who really wants to find out what the protagonist is going to do next to overcome their latest difficulty or challenge.

Mostly, you should concentrate on depicting characters interacting, with opposing goals, desires, and agendas, and on maintaining a forward momentum that keeps the story going at a fairly brisk pace. Adding a lot of unnecessary filler at a moment of action can be irritating and even laughable.

**More examples of overwriting:**

*Before:*

"That's not true, and you know it." Norman walked angrily across the moss-green thickly carpeted floor of his sunlit corner office, ignoring the shelves of well-worn books that lined the walls as he picked up the brass-framed sepia-toned photo that adorned the top of the mahogany desk that had been his father's and grandfather's. "Here's the proof!"

*After:*

"That's not true, and you know it." Norman crossed his office and picked up a framed photo from his desk. "Here's the proof!"

*Or:*

"That's not true, and you know it." Norman strode to his desk and snatched up a framed photo. "Here's the proof!"

And here's another example, disguised, from an author submission I received several years ago:

Hunched over the leather-covered steering wheel of his roadster, Harold Edmundson tore his weary eyes from the serpentine, shadowed road ahead to glance at the round dashboard clock; it was twenty minutes to ten.

He had barely moved an inch from the rigid driving position throughout the three-hour motorway journey, and now his tall, lean, muscular physique was craving release from its confinement in the metal cage of the sports car. In a deft movement of his tan leather gloved hand, he unfurled the black bow tie and unbuttoned the starched white collar. He massaged his stiff neck, tense shoulders, and aching back against the cream leather seat and stretched out his numbed arms against the wheel.

The windscreen wipers labored like a pair of frenzied metronomes to clear his vision for what lay ahead of him, but this landscape was indelibly marked in his mind. He could readily anticipate its twists and turns and trickeries as he had charted this dénouement in his dreams, day and night, for years.

And here's an example of over-the-top purple prose in a romance:

He gazed at her waves of daffodil-colored tresses tumbling over her alabaster skin, framing her heart-shaped face, her smooth neck and ample breasts a portrait of haunting beauty. He devoured the image before him: the sparkling azure eyes with lush lashes, the glossy cupid bow beseeching his kiss, the graceful contours of her neck and shoulders that led his gaze down to the fulsome orbs and inflamed buds of her breasts.

Overcome with the need to touch her, he stroked her silken hair and caressed her downy skin. He covered her rosebud lips with his and kissed her, first tenderly then ravenously, capturing her tongue in his, drawing her into him.

Most readers will find this kind of extreme writing laughable.

Just as rich foods and ultra-sweet desserts can be satisfying and enjoyable in small quantities, but too much will make us feel ill; rich descriptive passages (but not to the extreme of the last example) can work well in certain instances that warrant them. But they should be used sparingly, only where the situation warrants, and should be surrounded by sparser text for relief and to emphasize their significance.

For example, at a moment of high tension in your suspense novel, where any object in the scene could play a crucial role, you'll want to capture the reader's attention by showing every little detail along with the protagonist, who is desperately searching for a way to survive. Then later, when he recovers and is on to the next adventure, you'll pick up the pace again and describe his movements more sparsely and succinctly.

Or, if you're writing romance, perhaps you'll want a denser scene with lots of sensory imagery at a poignant moment. But even there, be careful not to overdo it. And pick up the pace again afterward.

One of the most important skills a writer can develop is the ability to convey a lot with an economy of words. So the delete key is your friend. Be sure to save your document in a new file first, or cut and paste the deleted bits to another file.

How can you tell if your writing style is overblown or not? Read a lot of popular fiction, especially in the genre you want to write. Compare your descriptive passages with theirs. If your passage seems wordier or more flowery, consider eliminating some of the excess verbiage.

It's all about trimming the fat to allow readers room to breathe and a chance to grasp the essence of your meaning; then they can fill in any details themselves. Also, readers don't want to be bludgeoned over the head with exaggerated reactions and emotions that dictate to them how to feel. They'd prefer to decide for themselves how they're going to react to what's going on in your story.

But, of course, don't go to the other extreme and make your writing too stark, laconic, or clinical. You do want to bring your characters and scenes to life for the readers, and that entails describing the surroundings and showing character's reactions to others and the environment. So vivid descriptions and skillful phrasing definitely have their place. Some adjectives and a few adverbs here and there are fine, as are some similes and metaphors – but in moderation. It's usually best to err on the side of simplicity. And remember, story trumps all.

**Concrete tips for dealing with overwritten passages or purple prose:**

~ Focus on the actual story – the struggles of the character to survive or reach her goal.

~ Cut out or condense the kinds of passages readers tend to skip.

~ Go through every scene to see if it should be cut or reduced and perhaps combined with another scene, or even summed up in a sentence or two.

~ Revisit any lengthy descriptions. Your depictions of scenes and people should be filtered through your character's viewpoint, and only elements that are relevant to the scene and their experience of the moment should be included. Leave extensive descriptions of scenery for travelogues. As Sally Carpenter says, "Be stingy when describing scenery or objects. You're giving snapshots, not selling real estate. Most readers won't wade through detailed descriptions." ("Overwriting – Less is More" in Five Scribes blog)

~ Similarly, keep descriptions of characters to a minimum. Paint with broad brushstrokes, highlighting physical attributes that affect their character or personality or life, and let readers fill in the unimportant details. And color the descriptions through the viewpoint and attitude of the character who is observing them.

~ Cut back on lengthy introspective moments where the story gets pushed aside and stalls out.

~ Avoid too much telling, describing, and explaining to the readers as the author. Show character actions and reactions in real time instead.

~ But don't go to the other extreme and show every minor or transitional scene in minute detail. Summarize unimportant scenes in a sentence or two and move on. Or just jump directly to the next important scene.

~ Cut back on literary devices like metaphors, similes, alliteration and other figurative language that distract the reader and scream, "Aren't I clever?" Use them judiciously, in more leisurely, thoughtful scenes.

~ Don't overdo or belabor character emotional reactions. Understated is often more powerful. Make sure your character reactions and feelings aren't exaggerated in relation to the actual event.

~ Don't overexplain or say the same thing in two or three different ways. Trust the readers to get it the first time.

~ "Kill your darlings" – those lovely passages you've slaved over and love, but that just don't fit in this story for one reason or other.

171

Cut them here and save them in a file called "extras" or "for future use" or whatever.

Don't have nonstop intense action. Give your readers a breather from time to time. If your powerful words and scenes are going to get a chance to have the desired effect on the reader, they need time to work before the next intense scene. Even in thrillers, the hero needs an opportunity to catch his breath and work out his next step.

**Specific tips:**

~ Avoid excessive use of adjectives and especially adverbs. (To flag adverbs, do a search for –ly words.) Instead, search for strong, precise nouns and verbs.

~ Replace distracting dialogue tags like "he chortled" and "she reiterated" with "he said" and "she said."

~ Replace esoteric, conspicuous, or abstract words with concrete, exact words that readers will immediately associate with the imagery and mood you're trying to convey. Don't jolt readers out of your story by making them go to the dictionary or even stop and wonder what a word means. You've lost instant communication and interrupted their reading experience. Remember that the primary purpose of writing is to communicate, and immediate comprehension is the ideal way to communicate. "The fact that no one understands you doesn't make you an artist." (Author unknown)

~ Pare down any wordiness or overblown language in dialogue. If a character goes on for more than about three sentences, break it up. Also, people don't tend to speak in complete, well-constructed sentences, especially in casual conversation.

~ Go through your manuscript paragraph by paragraph, word by word, and ask yourself if every word is contributing to the mood and driving the story forward. If not, cut it. Ideally, many words, especially descriptions of characters and setting, should do double duty. Besides describing a person or object, the words and phrases should also enhance the characterization, tone, and mood, and even add dissonance and tension.

*Incubate*

~ Put your manuscript away for a week or two, then read it aloud to see where you've maybe gone on for too long or used overblown language where simple, direct language would serve that scene better.

~ Lean language is especially important for tense scenes or anywhere you want fast pacing. Don't commit the beginners' faux-pas of describing the scenery while the character is running for her life!

For quieter, reflective scenes (and make sure you don't have too many of these, as you do want to maintain the narrative drive), feel free to enrich your prose with more "literary" descriptions and thoughtful moments. But be careful not to cross the line into overblown purple prose that will have savvy readers snickering.

As Mary Kole so aptly puts it, "...sometimes the simplest way of saying something – a way that's still artful and expressive but also restrained – is the best. When you're trying to show off in the prose, you lose sight of your real purpose: to tell a tale. When you're trying to be understood through multiple images and repetition, you're not giving your reader enough credit. Overwriting is all about trying too hard. Simplicity is all about letting the craft and the story speak for themselves." ("Two Signs of Overwriting and Why It's a Problem")

So don't muddy the waters – let your story shine through. Get out your red pen or click on the delete button and get rid of all extraneous description, over-the-top language, and anything else that doesn't support the story. The most important task of the revising and editing process is to ensure that every word is the best one for that spot.

Write directly, and just tell the story. Strive for clarity and a forward momentum.

173

# Chapter 27 – Adding Tension, Suspense, and Intrigue

All genres of fiction, not only thrillers, suspense novels, and action-adventure stories, need tension, suspense, and intrigue to keep readers engaged and interested. And of course, you'll need to ratchet up the tension and suspense a lot more if you're writing a fast-paced, nail-biting page-turner.

## A. GENERAL "BIG-PICTURE" TECHNIQUES:

## PLANNING:

**~ Create a protagonist we'll care about.**

Give your main character some secrets, regrets, and a fault or two, then get right into his head, preferably in the first paragraph of your story.

**~ Put your character in motion right away**.

Create an opening disturbance of some kind, preferably on the first page. Something negative happens to shake up his world or get in the way of a main goal. He needs to take action.

**~ Establish a sense of urgency, a tension-filled mood, and generally fast pacing.**

For suspense fiction, set a tense tone right from the start. Unlike cozy mysteries and other more leisurely genres, thrillers and other suspense fiction need an anxious mood and fast pacing throughout most of the novel, with short "breathers" in between the most gripping scenes.

### ~ Threaten your protagonist.

Create a significant, meaningful, overarching story problem, preferably a threat with far-reaching consequences. To increase the stakes and reader worry, make it personal to your protagonist. He and his loved ones are personally threatened.

Create an overriding sentence about this to keep in mind as you're writing your story:

Will (name) survive / stop / find / overcome (ordeal/person/difficulty/threat) on time to save himself or others?

Here's a premise in a nutshell for a gripping, entertaining story your readers will love:

(Hero or heroine's name) wants ... (what will complete their life, make them happy, fulfill their main goal, satisfy their biggest hope or desire?). But he/she is hampered by ... (describe the misfortune, conflict, dilemma, problem, villain), and s/he has ... (time limit or other hindrance) to ... (describe the almost impossible task) or ... (describe a negative consequence that will happen). He/she has to choose between... and .... (Continue from there.)

### ~ Create a worthy opponent for your protagonist.

You also need some significant opposition to your character and his goals. Who or what is preventing him from realizing his hopes and dreams? Or even directly threatening him or someone close to him? Or other innocent people? Who's responsible for upsetting his world and forcing him to take action?

You should have a nasty, cunning, determined antagonist. Your villain needs to be as intelligent, motivated, and resourceful as your protagonist – or even more so. Make him or her a serious force to be reckoned with.

But don't make your villain a one-dimensional cardboard caricature. Make him complex and multi-dimensional, too.

175

Remember, your villain justifies his actions and thinks of himself as the hero of the story.

## WRITING:

### ~ Show, don't tell.

Show all your critical scenes in real time as they're happening, with action, reaction, and dialogue. Show your main character's inner feelings and physical and emotional reactions. Don't have one character tell another about an important event or scene. (See the chapters on this.)

### ~ Use multiple viewpoints, especially that of the villain.

For increased anxiety and suspense, get us into the head of your antagonist from time to time. This way the readers find out critical information the heroine doesn't know, things we want to warn her about!

### ~ Keep the story momentum moving forward.

Don't get bogged down in backstory or exposition. Keep the action moving ahead, especially in the first chapter. Then work in background details and other info little by little, on an "as-needed" basis only, through dialogue or flashbacks – not as the author telling the readers.

### ~ Set the mood & tone with vivid imagery.

Use the setting to establish the mood and create suspense. This is the equivalent of the ominous atmosphere, harsh lighting, strange camera angles, or nasty weather in a scary movie.

Avoid light, cheery words or upbeat imagery at tense times.

For example, your characters are racing through the forest, trying desperately to get away from their pursuers, who are out to kill them. Don't tell us about the sun peeking through the trees, the bunny rabbit hopping by, the birds twittering, or the brook babbling. Give us nasty weather, darkness, discomfort, and danger – a threatening, scary environment.

In general, make sure all your word choices add to the tension, rather than detracting from it. Don't have your character *strolling* or *relaxing* or *lounging*. Have him *striding* or *hurrying* or *pacing the floor* or *hunched over*, peering at his computer screen.

~ **Create a mood of unease** by showing the main character feeling apprehensive about something or someone or by revealing some of the bad guy's thoughts and intentions.

Also use compelling, vivid sensory imagery to take us right there, with the protagonist, experiencing and reacting to whoever or whatever is challenging or threatening her. To make the reader feel right there, appeal to as many senses as possible, not just sights and sounds. Scents, for example, are often powerful and evocative.

~ **Pile on the problems. Hamper your hero or heroine at every turn.**

A worried reader is an engaged reader. Keep your readers on the edge of their seats, turning the pages. I'll get into some specific ways later in this chapter.

~ **Put some tension and conflict in every scene.**

There should be something unresolved in every scene. Your character enters the scene with an objective or agenda, but she encounters obstacles in the scene, so she is thwarted in her efforts to reach her goal.

~ **Every page needs tension.**

Put some tension on every page. It doesn't necessarily need to be a fight or argument or even overt disagreement. It can be discomfort, uneasiness, pain, anxiety, anticipation, impatience, or worry. Or inner conflict, resentments, questioning, or doubt.

Even if you have two good friends or close family members talking, give them opposing agendas to add tension. Make either the topic critical in some way or show inner or outer discord of some kind.

### ~ But do vary the tension.

Of course, you can't keep up tension nonstop, as it's tiring for readers and will eventually numb them. It's best to intersperse tense, nail-biting scenes with a few more leisurely, relaxed scenes (but not too laid-back) that provide a bit of a reprieve before the next tense, harrowing scene starts.

### ~ Dialogue is war.

Your dialogue should be like conversation in real life, but on steroids. Skip the Hi, how are you? Nice weather, yadda, yadda stuff and jump right to the heart of the matter.

### ~ Add in tough choices and moral dilemmas.

Devise ongoing difficult decisions and inner conflict for your lead character. Besides making your plot more suspenseful, this will also make your protagonist more complex, vulnerable, and intriguing.

### ~ Add contradictions and layers.

Show your POV character's reactions and inner thoughts, especially if they contradict what he or she is saying. Also, show the other person's body language to add layers of meaning.

### ~ Keep raising the stakes.
Keep asking yourself, "How can I make things worse for the protagonist?" As the challenges get more difficult and the obstacles more insurmountable, readers worry more and suspense grows. When or if he resolves one issue, add another, worse one. If the main problems are solved, the reader feels she can stop reading the book. Introduce the next problem or complication at the end of the current scene – or at least hint at it.

Your plot should be like a jagged graph line, with ups and downs, but continually rising until it reaches the climax, then it drops to the final resolution.

# B. ADVANCED TECHNIQUES & DEVICES TO ADD SUSPENSE & INTRIGUE

## DELAYS & INTERRUPTIONS ADD SUSPENSE

~ **Provide an incomplete, tantalizing picture.** Withhold critical information. Don't tell your readers too much too soon. Dole out information little by little, to tantalize readers and keep them wondering. Keep details of the past of both your protagonist and antagonist hidden, and hint at critical, life-altering experiences they've had that are impacting their present goals, desires, fears, etc. Add one tiny detail after another as you go along, or maybe a short flashback here and there. Reveal the truth little by little, like shadowy veils being removed one at a time.

~ **Delay answers to critical plot questions.** Look for places in your story where you've answered readers' questions too soon, so have missed a prime spot to increase tension and suspense. Draw out the time before answering that question. In the meantime, hint at it from time to time to remind readers of its importance.

~ **Interrupt a scene at a critical moment – leave the readers thirsting for more.** Make your character desperate to reveal key information to someone (and us), but something prevents or cuts off her confession. Perhaps the phone rings or someone knocks at the door, or her child wakes up and starts calling for her.

~ **Stretch out critical or scary scenes – milk them for all they're worth.** Your hero is trapped in a locked shed. They're coming back for him soon. As his eyes adjust to the dim light, he desperately looks around him for anything that could help him get out before they come back. Move the camera in close and show each thing he looks at and considers. Stretch out those crucial seconds as he races against time to save himself.

## USE CLIFFHANGERS & JUMP CUTS

~ **Cliffhangers leave the readers hanging** – and keep them turning the pages.

179

End your chapter or scene at a critical, dangerous, nail-biting moment for the main character, in order to keep readers on the edge of their seats and compel them to continue to the next chapter to find out what happens.

~ **Jump cuts add even more suspense & intrigue.** You end with a cliffhanger, then the next scene starts with different characters in a different place. Then you end that one at a critical point and go back to the previous scene, where you continue on with those characters.

## BRAINSTORM FOR SOME TWISTS & REVERSALS

~ **Plan a few plot twists.** Add in some surprising information or unexpected developments. Readers are surprised and delighted when the events take a turn they never expected. Don't let your readers become complacent, thinking it's easy to figure out the ending, or they may stop reading.

Try for a big twist in the middle and one at the end. What will readers expect to happen next? Brainstorm a lot of possibilities that readers won't expect, then choose one.

~ **Add in some reversals of feelings, attitudes, or expectations.** The character changes her mind and decides to do something radically different.

## USE MULTIPLE VIEWPOINTS

To increase tension and suspense, in a few chapters here and there, show the point of view, thoughts, and scheming of the villain or other antagonist. The main character doesn't have this info, but the readers do. This way, readers find out how clever, determined, and nasty the antagonist is and start worrying about the hero or heroine. But be sure to stay in the bad guy's head for that whole scene. Or if you have a change in point of view within a scene, leave a blank space first, and only do that once.

This allows you to use **dramatic irony**, where your readers know something critical and scary that the protagonist is not aware of. For example, your heroine is relaxing after a stressful day, unaware that the killer is prying open her basement window.

## USE FORESHADOWING TO INCITE CURIOSITY

**Tease the readers with innuendos.** Drop subtle hints of troubles to come. Hint at the main character's past secrets. What is the character worried about or afraid might happen? Capitalize on this.

Foreshadowing is about sprinkling in subtle little hints and clues as you go along about possible revelations, complications, and trouble to come. It incites curiosity, anticipation, and worry in the readers, which is exactly what you want. So to pique the readers' interest and keep them absorbed, be sure to continually hint at possible dangers lurking ahead.

But do be subtle about your little hints. If you make them too obvious, it takes away the suspense and intrigue, along with the reader's satisfaction at trying to figure everything out.

Foreshadowing is also great for revealing character traits, flaws, phobias, weaknesses, and secrets. You do this by briefly alluding to the character's secret, worry, or fear.

For more specific tips for foreshadowing, see my book, *Writing a Killer Thriller*.

## REVELATIONS & EPIPHANIES

Revelations are when character secrets and other critical information are revealed at strategic moments. Perhaps where something is hidden, a secret child shows up, or whatever.

Use brief flashbacks at key moments to reveal your main character's childhood traumas, unpleasant events, secrets, emotional baggage, hangups, dysfunctional family, etc.

Or perhaps the lead or another central character has an epiphany or two – a "Eureka!" or "Ah-ha!" moment. "Of course! Why didn't I think of that before!" But make sure it's not something readers will have already thought of – you want your character to be astute and as sharp as, or quicker than, most readers.

## KEEP HAMPERING YOUR HERO OR HEROINE THROUGHOUT THE NOVEL

Your hero might be hindered by:

~ **A ticking clock** – every second is critical to stop the villain before he kills or for the hero to escape being killed.

~ **Obstacles, hindrances** – the door is locked, there's a police roadblock, or whatever.

~ **Pursuers** – he is being chased.

~ **Traps, restrictions** – she's locked in; he's fallen down a deep hole trap in the jungle; they're tied up in a basement, and so on.

~ **Handicaps, injuries** – she twists her ankle, he's temporarily blinded, they've been hurt in a car crash, etc.

~ **Bad luck** – he drops his gun into the ocean; the small plane crashes; the road is icy and the car goes over a cliff, or ...

## CREATE A BREATHTAKING CLIMAX

~ **Create a darkest moment** for the hero or heroine, where they're faced with the ultimate challenge. He or she has to call on every drop of reserve energy, wits, strength, courage and determination to get through it.

~ **Devise a heart-pounding showdown scene**, a very close life-or-death "battle." And by the way "death" doesn't have to mean physical death – can be psychological or professional.

~ **Create a surprise twist near the end.** Leave the reader with "Omigod!" But the plot twist has to actually make sense if they go back through all the details of the story.

~ **Let your hero win by his own devices.** Don't have a *Deus ex machina* – act of God – or a supporting character saving the day. Or the villain backing down and conceding. The hero or heroine has to win through his own determination and major effort. Readers have been rooting for the hero all through the story, so don't let them down by having him saved by something or someone else – let him be the one to beat the odds, vanquish the enemy, and save innocent lives.

## Create a MEMORABLE, SATISFYING ENDING

Give the readers relief from the tension and some sense of satisfaction that the hero or heroine they've been rooting for survives and wins. Also, show a character arc and some inner growth. The experiences of the story have changed the character.

Also, be sure all prior details now make sense.

Finally, leave the readers with some resonance by giving them a memorable ending that stays with them for a while, gives them something to think about.

## GO BACK AND TIGHTEN YOUR WRITING FOR THE WHOLE STORY

Make every chapter, scene, page, paragraph, sentence, and word count. See my book, *Fire up Your Fiction*, for lots of concrete tips with examples for revising your novel or short story to make it more compelling.

# PART VII

# OVERVIEW, CHECKLISTS, ADDITIONAL TIPS

# Chapter 28 – A Checklist for Writing Fiction Readers Can't Put Down

Here's a blueprint for writing short stories and novels that will engage and delight readers – and garner great reviews. Keep this checklist handy as you're planning, writing, and revising your story.

*Note that "YES" is the answer you're always striving for here.

For concrete advice with examples on how to achieve each of these results, see specific topics in the rest of this book and also in my other two books, *Fire up Your Fiction* and *Writing a Killer Thriller*.

## PLANNING STAGE:

__ Have I zeroed in on a genre and target readership?

__ Have I established an interesting story world (setting)?

__ Have I created a significant story question, problem, or challenge?

__ Have I created some interesting, unique, even quirky characters to populate my story?

__ Have I chosen one main character (protagonist), the person with the most at stake in the story and the one readers will most want to identify with and root for?

__ Does my protagonist have a significant goal or desire that's strong enough to make him fight for it through the whole story?

__ Is someone or something standing in the way of my protagonist reaching his or her goal?

__ Can I state my storyline in 35 words or less? Include the genre, lead character, and main problem for that character.

__ Is my main character (protagonist) unique, complex, and memorable?

__ Is my protagonist likeable enough or fascinating enough for readers to want to spend a whole novel avidly following and identifying with him or her?

__ Have I given my main character a flaw, vulnerability, or shameful secret to make him more complex and add interest and worry?

__ Does my protagonist have some opposing, conflicting desires, convictions or goals that will create inner conflict and indecision?

__ Is the antagonist or villain "worthy" of the role of main opposition to the protagonist?

__ Does the antagonist have both strengths and weaknesses?

__ Have I made my antagonist or villain unique, cunning, powerful, determined, and a force to be reckoned with?

__ Have I made my antagonist multi-faceted and interesting by giving him a positive attribute or two?

__ Have I created an interesting, quirky sidekick, best friend, sibling, colleague, or other supporting character?

__ Is the sidekick, sibling, or BFF different from the protagonist, for contrast?

__ If this is a romance or story with romantic elements, have I created an attractive, charismatic love interest?

## WRITING STAGE

__ Do I have an enticing hook on the first page and inciting incident on the first few pages?

__ Do I open with an active opening scene involving my main character and another character or two?

\_\_ Have I situated readers right from the beginning of Chapter 1 so they know *who, what, where,* and *when*?

\_\_When describing the immediate environment (setting), am I bringing it to life by showing it through the point of view of the main character, with his or her personal observations, reactions, sensory sensations, and attitudes?

\_\_ Have I made sure setting details are relevant to what's happening at that moment, and not a distraction?

\_\_ Have I avoided interrupting the story line with lengthy background information (backstory), all in one chunk?

\_\_ Instead, am I marbling only the necessary or relevant information in small bits through the first third or half of the novel?

\_\_ Is my protagonist actively involved in his or her fate and showing courage and initiative, rather than passively reacting to situations?

\_\_ Am I mostly "showing," with scenes in real time, with action, tension, and dialogue, rather than "telling" readers about something that already occurred?

\_\_ Am I coloring descriptions of other characters through the viewpoint character's observations and attitudes?

\_\_ Do my character descriptions also reveal personality and motivations? Rather than imposing a laundry list of items of physical attributes and clothing, have I allowed readers to fill in the blanks as they choose?

\_\_ Am I bringing my scenes to life with concrete details and precise, evocative language, rather than vague generalizations and abstract ideas?

\_\_ Am I using sensory imagery to engage readers, including sounds, smells, tactile sensations, and taste, as well as visual experiences?

187

__ Am I heightening reader interest and engagement by creating tension on almost every page, and conflict and change in every scene?

__ Have I taken care not to bore readers with lengthy rumination, analysis, explanations, descriptions, or background?

__ Have I tried to stay out of the story, to avoid inserting annoying author intrusions?

__ Have I increased/maintained reader intrigue and anticipation by hinting at critical information (foreshadowing), but holding back on the details as long as possible?

__ In my dialogue, have I broken up any long monologues into questions and answers with disagreement and attitude?

__ Is my dialogue generally short and snappy, with partial sentences, one or two-word questions and responses, and plenty of tension?

__ Does each character speak differently, depending on their gender, personality, and background?

__ Is most of the narrative in the main character's voice, too?

__ Have I delayed resolutions of the protagonist's problems to keep readers worrying and turning the pages?

__ As my novel progresses, have I continually added greater obstacles, dilemmas, and challenges?

__ Have I inserted a few twists and surprises to increase suspense?

__ Have I avoided telling readers how the characters feel and how they (the readers) should feel? Have I instead shown how the characters are feeling by their actions, reactions, words, facial expressions, and body language?

__ Am I staying mainly in the protagonist's point of view?

__ Am I staying in the viewpoint of only one character per scene?

__ Do I end my chapters with a question, worry, new dilemma, or some other kind of thruster to impel the reader to keep reading?

## REVISING STAGE

### Big-picture issues:

__ Are all my characters' motivations and actions believable and "in character"? Would those characters actually make those decisions, say and do those things in those situations, given their background and personality?

__ Have I searched for and addressed any plot holes, discrepancies, or inconsistencies in timeline or other details?

__ Are most of my scenes in "real time" (showing) with action and dialogue, rather than related after the fact (telling)?

__ Have I cut or revised any boring scenes without conflict that don't drive the story forward or contribute to characterization?

__ Have I shortened or cut boring paragraphs or passages to tighten my writing?

__ Have I cut down on lengthy narration and internal monologue between active scenes?

__ Have I sparked up any dull dialogue by making it more confrontational or adversarial? Or at least snappy, with attitude or humor?

__ Are there any scenes that I like but don't really fit in this story? Have I revised or deleted them? (Save them for another story.)

### Style editing:

### Weeding and tightening:

__ Have I checked for and deleted any repetitions of ideas, places where I've said the same thing two or three times, to pick up the pace and streamline my writing?

\_\_ Have I deleted any "little word pile-ups" and smoothed out my sentences for better flow and rhythm?

\_\_ Have I made every word count? Are there still some excess or repetitive phrases or words I can delete to tighten my writing and make the scenes more compelling?

**Editing for consistent, fresh style:**

\_\_ Verb tenses – is all the action in the past (or present) tense, rather than jumping back and forth between "was" and "is," "were" and "are," "saw" and "sees," "said" and "says," etc?

\_\_ Have I replaced overdone "vanilla" verbs like *walked, ran, looked, spoke* with fresh, strong, specific ones like *bolted, stumbled, trudged*, etc.?

\_\_ Have I replaced ordinary verbs plus supporting adverbs with stronger verbs? Replace "she spoke quietly" with "she whispered." Replace "he ran quickly" with "he hurried" or "he raced" or "he sprinted" or "he darted," etc.

\_\_ Have I taken out wishy-washy qualifiers like *quite, sort of, kind of, somewhat, a bit*, and *fairly*, which lessen the impact and dilute my prose? Instead of "The rapids looked kind of treacherous," say "The rapids looked treacherous, even for an expert."

\_\_ Have I taken out most instances of "very" and replaced the *very* plus adjective with a stronger, more precise adjective? (For example, instead of "very tall" say "towering.")

\_\_ Have I checked for repeating the same noun or adjective several times within a page? For variety and a fresh feeling, find alternate wording for most of them.

\_\_ Have I checked for any clichés and found a fresh, novel way to express that idea? (Some clichés are fine in dialogue, if they add to unique or quirky characterization, especially for older people.)

\_\_ Have I done a search "Find and Replace" for any pet words I tend to overuse, and deleted or replaced most of them?

190

## Dialogue:

__ Does my dialogue sound authentic? Or is it stilted, too correct sounding? Read it aloud or role-play scenes with a friend.

__ Does my dialogue include enough tension? Take out any banal, ho-hum comments.

__ Have I eliminated any overly correct sentences and replaced formal words with casual ones in my dialogue?

__ Rather than dialogue tags that draw attention to themselves like "he expostulated" or "she reiterated," have I mainly used the almost invisible "he said" and "she said" with my dialogue?

__ Have I avoided "talking heads" and created visuals to situate the speakers by using action tags with my dialogue, like "She hung up her coat" or "He poured some coffee."

## Final proofreading:

__ Have I broken up any long paragraphs?

__ Do I have a question mark at the end of all questions?

__ Have I used exclamation marks sparingly, reserving them for a character screaming, shouting, shocked, delighted or triumphant, or in pain?

__ Do I have quotation marks around all dialogue?

__ Have I dropped to a new paragraph for every new speaker?

__ Have I started a new paragraph for another character reacting to the speaker?

## Chapter 29 – 33 Tips for Creating a Short Story Worthy of Contests, Magazines, and Anthologies

Writing short stories is an excellent way to test the waters of fiction without making a huge commitment, or to experiment with different genres, characters, settings, and voices.

Even if you've published a novel or two, it's a good idea to try to release a few high-quality, well-edited short stories between books to help with discoverability and growing a fan base.

Also, today's busy readers (especially the young ones) have more distractions and temptations for their time, therefore shorter attention spans, and they're reading on smaller devices, so a short story is a perfect escapism-byte for increasing numbers of people.

As blogger and author Anne R. Allen said in an excellent article in Writer's Digest magazine, "Bite-sized fiction has moved mainstream, and today's readers are more eager than ever to 'read short.'" To check out Anne's "nine factors working in favor of a short story renaissance," see "9 Ways Writing Short Stories Can Pay off For Writers," and there's more in her post, "Why You Should be Writing Short Fiction."

### HOW TO WRITE A WINNING SHORT STORY

Here are 33 concrete tips for writing a compelling short story that is worthy of publishing or submitting to contests, magazines, and anthologies. Of course, these are only guidelines – like any good cook with a recipe, you'll tweak them to suit your own vision, goal, genre, and story idea.

When referring to the main character, I'll be alternating between using "he" and "she", so just fill in the gender of your own protagonist.

## PLANNING STAGE:

1. **Keep the story tight.** Most short stories are between 1,000 and 7,000 words long, with the most popular length between 2,500 and 4,000 words. Unlike a novel or even a novella, a short story is about a small slice of life, with one story thread and one theme. Don't get too ambitious. It's best to limit it to one principal character plus a few supporting characters, one main conflict, one geographical location, and a brief time frame, like a few weeks maximum – better yet, a few days, or even hours.

2. **Create a main character who is complex and charismatic, one readers will care about.** Your protagonist should be multi-dimensional and at least somewhat sympathetic, so readers can relate to him and start bonding with him right away. He should be fascinating, with plenty of personality. But give him a human side, with some inner conflict and vulnerability, so readers identify with him and start worrying about him immediately. If readers don't care about your character, they also won't care about what happens to him.

3. **Give your protagonist a burning desire.** What does he or she want more than anything? This is the basis for your story goal, the driving force of your story.

4. **Decide what your character is most afraid of.** What does your heroine regret most? What is she feeling guilty about? Give her some baggage and secrets.

5. **Devise a critical story problem or conflict.** Create a significant conflict or challenge for your protagonist. Put her in hot water right away, on the first page, so the readers start worrying about her early on. No conflict = no story. The conflict can be internal, external, or interpersonal, or all three. It can be against one's own demons, other people, circumstances, or nature.

6. **Develop a unique "voice" for this story.** First, get to know your character really well by journaling in his voice. Pretend you are the character, writing in his secret diary, expressing his hopes and fears

and venting his frustrations. Just let the ideas flow, in his point of view, using his words and expressions.

Then take it a step further and carry that voice you've developed throughout the whole story, even to the narration and description, which are really the viewpoint character's thoughts, perceptions, observations, and reactions. This technique ensures that your whole story has a unique, compelling voice. (In a novel, the voice will of course change in any chapters that are in other characters' viewpoints.)

7. **Create a worthy antagonist.** Devise an opposition character who is strong, clever, determined, and resourceful – a force to be reckoned with. And for added interest, make him or her multi-faceted, with a few positive qualities, too.

8. **Add in a few interesting, even quirky supporting characters.** Give each of your characters a distinct personality, with their own agenda, hopes, accomplishments, fears, insecurities, and secrets, and add some individual quirks to bring each of them to life. Supporting and minor characters should be quite different from your protagonist, for contrast. Start a diary for each important character to develop their voice and personality, and ensure none of them are closely modeled after you, the author, or your friends.

But don't fully develop any very minor or "walk-on" characters, or readers will expect them to play a more significant role. In fact, it's best not to name minor characters like cab drivers, cashiers, and servers, unless they play a bigger role.

9. **To enter and win contests, make your character and story unique and memorable.** Try to jolt or awe the readers somehow, with a unique, enigmatic, even quirky or weird character; an unusual premise or situation; and an unexpected, even shocking revelation and plot twist.

10. **Experiment – take a chance.** Short stories can be edgier, darker, or more intense because they're brief, and readers can tolerate something a little more extreme for a limited time.

**WRITING STAGE:**

11. **Start with a compelling scene.** Short stories need to grab and emotionally engage the readers right from the first paragraph. Don't open with a description of the scenery or other setting. Also, don't start with background information (backstory) on the character or an explanation of their world or situation.

12. **Start right out in the head of your main character.** It's best to use his name right in the first sentence to establish him as the point-of-view character, the one readers are supposed to identify with and root for. And let readers know really soon his rough age, situation, and role in the story world.

13. **Put your character in motion right away.** Having her interacting with someone else is usually best – much more dynamic than starting with a character alone, musing. Also, it's best not to start with your character waking up or in an everyday situation or on the way to somewhere. That's trite and too much of a slow lead-up for a short story – or any compelling story, for that matter.

14. **Use close point of view.** Get up close and personal with your lead character and tell the whole story from his point of view. Continually show his thoughts, feelings, reactions, and physical sensations. And take care not to show anyone else's thoughts or inner reactions. You don't have time or space to get into anyone else's viewpoint in a short story. Show the attitudes and reactions of others through what the POV character perceives – their words, body language, facial expressions, tone of voice, actions, etc.

Even the narration should be expressed as your POV character's thoughts and observations. Don't intrude as the author to describe or explain anything to the readers in neutral language. You want to keep your readers immersed in your fictive dream, and interrupting as the author will burst the bubble of make-believe they crave.

15. **Situate the reader early on**. To avoid audience confusion and frustration, establish your main character immediately and clarify the situation and setting (time and place) within the first few

paragraphs. On the first page, answer the four W's: *who, what, where, when.* But as mentioned above, avoid starting with a long descriptive passage.

16. **Jump right in with some tension in the first paragraphs.** As I mentioned, there's no room in a short story for a long, meandering lead-up to the main problem, or an extended description of the setting or the characters and their background. Disrupt the main character's life in some way on the first page. As Kurt Vonnegut advises, in short fiction, start as close to the end as possible.

17. **Show, don't tell.** Don't use narration to tell your readers what happened – put them right in the middle of the scene, with lots of dialogue and action and reactions, in real time. And skip past transitional times and unimportant moments. Use a few words to go from one time or place to another, unless something important happens during the transition.

18. **Your character needs to react.** Continually show your character's emotional and physical reactions, both inner and outer, to what's going on around him. And to bring the character and scene to life on the page, evoke as many of the five senses as possible, not just sight and hearing. Scents or smells are especially powerful and evocative.

19. **Every page needs tension of some sort.** It might be overt, like an argument, or subtle, like inner resentments, disagreements, questioning, or anxiety. If everybody is in agreement, shake things up a little.

20. **To add tension and intrigue, withhold key information,** especially about character secrets or regrets, but hint at them to arouse reader curiosity. Then reveal critical info bit by bit, like a tantalizing striptease, as you go along.

21. **Dialogue in fiction is like real conversation on steroids.** Skip the yadda-yadda, blah-blah. "How are you? I'm fine. Nice weather," etc., and add spark and tension to all your dialogue. And make the characters' words and expressions sound as natural and

authentic as you can. Avoid complete, correct sentences in dialogue. Use plenty of one or two-word questions and responses, evasive replies, abrupt changes of topics, and even a few silences.

22. **Each character should speak differently, and not like the author.** Each character's word choices and speech patterns should reflect their gender, age, education, social standing, and personality. Don't have your kids sounding like adults or your thugs sounding like university professors. Even men and women of similar cultural backgrounds and social standing speak differently. Read your dialogue out loud or role-play with a friend to make sure it sounds real, has tension, and moves along at a good clip.

23. **Build the conflict to a riveting climax.** Keep putting your protagonist in more hot water until the big "battle," showdown, or struggle – whether it's physical, psychological, or interpersonal. This is where they're challenged to the max and have to draw on all their courage, wit, and resources to avoid defeat and/or reach their goals.

24. **Brainstorm to devise a twist at the end.** Create a surprise ending to delight readers – something that's unexpected but makes sense in retrospect. Give the readers what they hope for, but not in a way they expect it.

25. **Provide some satisfaction at the end.** It's not necessary to tie everything up in a neat little bow, but do give your readers some sense of resolution, some payout for their investment of time and effort in your story. As in novels, most readers want the character they've been rooting for all along to resolve at least some of their problems. But be sure the protagonist they've been identifying with succeeds through their own courage, determination, and resourcefulness, not through coincidence, luck, or a rescue by someone else. Keep your hero or heroine heroic. And don't let your conclusion drag on – tie things up quickly.

26. **Provide a character arc:** Your protagonist should have changed as a result of his recent struggles.

27. **And a story arc – how are things different?** How has the life of the main character changed as a result of what she's just been through?

**REVISION STAGE:**

28. **Hook 'em in right away.** Now that you've got your whole story down, go back and grab the readers with an opening that zings. Write and rewrite your first line, opening paragraph, and first page. They need to be as gripping and as intriguing as you can make them, in order to compel the readers to read the rest of the story. Your first sentence and paragraph should arouse curiosity and raise questions that demand to be answered.

29. **Cut to the chase. The short story requires discipline and editing.** Trim down any long, convoluted sentences to reveal the essentials. Less is more, so make every word count. If a paragraph, sentence, or line of dialogue doesn't advance the plot, add intrigue, or develop a character, take it out.

Also, use strong, evocative, specific nouns and verbs and cut back on supporting adjectives and adverbs. For example, instead of saying "He walked heavily" say "He stomped" or "He trudged." Or instead of "She walked quietly," say "She tiptoed" or "She crept."

30. **Make every element and every image count.** Every significant detail you insert in the story should have some significance or some relevance later. If it doesn't, take it out. Don't show us a knife or special character skills, for example, if they don't show up later and play an essential role. You have no room for filler or extraneous details in a compelling short story.

31. **Try to make all descriptions do double duty.** When you're describing a character, for example, rather than listing their physical attributes and what they're wearing, search for details that reveal their personality, their mood, their intentions, and their effect on those around them, and also the personality and attitude of the character who is observing them. And there's no need to go into

detail on everything they're wearing. Paint in bold brush strokes and let readers fill in the details – or not, as they prefer.

32. **Stay in character for all descriptions.** Filter all descriptions through the attitude and mood of the main character. If your POV character's aging father shows up at the door, don't describe him neutrally and in detail as a brand new character. Show him as that character actually sees her own father.

Similarly, if a teenage boy walks into a room, don't describe the space as an interior designer would see it – stay in his viewpoint. He is most concerned with why he entered that room, not all the details of what it looks like.

33. **Pay attention to word count and other guidelines.** As I mentioned earlier, short stories are generally between 1,000 and 7,500 words long, with the most popular length around 2,500 to 4,000 words. If you want to submit your short story to a website, magazine or contest, be sure to read their guidelines as to length, genre, language no-no's, and so on. Also, for your own protection, do read the fine print to avoid giving away all rights to your story.

# Chapter 30 – 15 Questions for Your Beta Readers – and to Focus Your Revisions

So you've completed the first draft of your novel? Congratulations! Now it's time to start the all-important revision process. Be sure not to shoot yourself in the foot by sending it off or self-publishing it too soon. That's the biggest mistake of unsuccessful novelists – being in too much of a hurry to get their book out, when it still needs (major or minor) revisions and final polishing.

To start, put it aside for a week or more, then change the font and print it up and read it in a different location, where you don't write. Or, to save paper, put it on your tablet and take it outside to a park or a (different) coffee shop to read. That way, you can approach it with fresh eyes and a bit of distance, as a reader, rather than in too close as the writer. Using the questions below to guide you, go through the whole manuscript for big-picture issues: logistics, characterization, plot, writing style, flow. Try to put some tension on every page, even if it's only minor internal disagreement. Remember that conflict and tension are what drive fiction forward. As you read, correct minor errors and typos that jump out at you and make notes in the margins and on the backs of the pages. Then go back to the computer and type in your changes.

Now it's time to seek out 3-6 avid readers to give you some feedback. It's best not to ask your parent, child, significant other, sibling, or BFF to do this "beta" reading, as they probably won't want to tell you what they really think, for fear of jeopardizing your relationship. Or they may be so critical it actually will hurt your relationship. Your volunteer readers don't need to be writers, but they should be smart, discerning readers who enjoy and read your genre, and are willing to give you honest feedback.

So how do you find your beta readers? Perhaps through a critique group, writing class, workshop, book club, writers' organization, or online networking such as Facebook, Twitter, or Google+. In the case of a YA novel or children's book, look around for be age-appropriate relatives, neighborhood kids, or the children of your friends – or perhaps you know a teacher or librarian who would be willing to read some or all of it aloud to students and collect feedback.

To avoid generic (and generally useless) responses like "I liked it," "It was good," or "It was okay," it's best to guide your readers with specific questions. Here's a list to choose from, based on suggestions from novelists I know. If you're hesitant to ask your volunteers so many questions, you could perhaps have them pick the ones that seem most relevant to your story and writing style. And of course, if you first use these questions as a guideline during your revisions, the responses from your beta readers should be much more positive, or of a nature to take your story and your skills up a level or two.

1. Did the story hold your interest from the very beginning? If not, why not?

2. Did you get oriented fairly quickly at the beginning as to whose story it is, and where and when it's taking place? If not, why not?

3. Could you relate to the main character? Did you feel her/his pain or excitement?

4. Did the setting interest you, and did the descriptions seem vivid and real to you?

5. Was there a point at which you felt the story started to lag or you became less than excited about finding out what was going to happen next? Where, exactly?

6. Were there any parts that confused you? Or even frustrated or annoyed you? Which parts, and why?

7. Did you notice any discrepancies or inconsistencies in time sequences, places, character details, or other aspects?

8. Were the characters believable? Are there any characters you think could be made more interesting or more likeable?

9. Did you get confused about who's who in the characters? Were there too many characters to keep track of? Too few? Are any of the names or characters too similar?

10. Did the dialogue keep your interest and seem natural to you? If not, whose dialogue did you think sounded artificial or not like that person would speak?

11. Did you feel there was too much description or exposition? Not enough? Maybe too much dialogue in parts?

12. Was there enough conflict, tension, and intrigue to keep your interest?

13. Was the ending satisfying? Believable?

14. Did you notice any obvious, repeating grammatical, spelling, punctuation or capitalization errors? Examples?

15. Do you think the writing style suits the genre? If not, why not?

And if you have eager readers or other writers in your genre who are willing to go the extra mile for you, you could add some of the more specific questions below. These are also good for critiquing a short story.

~ Which scenes/paragraphs/lines did you really like?

~ Which parts did you dislike or not like as much, and why?

~ Are there parts where you wanted to skip ahead or put the book down?

~ Which parts resonated with you and/or moved you emotionally?

~ Which parts should be condensed or even deleted?

~ Which parts should be elaborated on or brought more to life?

~ Are there any confusing parts? What confused you?

~ Which characters did you really connect to?

~ Which characters need more development or focus?

Once you've received feedback from all your beta readers, it's time to consider their comments carefully. Ignore any you really don't agree with, but if two or more people say the same thing, be sure to seriously consider that comment or suggestion. Now go through and revise your story, based on the comments you felt were insightful and helpful.

# Chapter 31 – 12 Essential Steps from Story Idea to Publish-Ready Novel

If you want your novel, novella, or short story to intrigue readers and garner great reviews, use these twelve steps to guide you along at each phase of the process:

1. **Brainstorm possibilities – or just start writing**. Make a story map/diagram to decide *who* (protagonist, antagonist, supporting characters), *what* (main problem), *where* (physical setting), and *when* (past, present future, season). Or start writing and see where it takes you – but be warned that this "pantser" method (writing by the seat of your pants) will require more time and effort editing, cutting, rearranging, and revising (and probably swearing, hair-pulling, and rewriting) later.

2. **Write with wild abandon while your muse is flowing.** At this first stage, don't stop to edit or rethink or revise anything. Just write, write, write. Don't show it to anyone and don't ask for advice. Try to write uncensored until you get all or most of the first draft of your story down. If you get blocked or discouraged, put your writing aside for a bit and go to step 3.

3. **At an impasse or run out of steam? Take a break and hone your skills.** Read some highly regarded, reader-friendly craft-of-writing books. See the list at the end of recommended resources for fiction writers. And maybe attend a few writing workshops or conferences or join a critique group. Also, read blog posts on effective writing techniques. See *The Write Life* blog or *Writer's Digest* magazine for a list of the 100 Best Blogs for Writers.

4. **First revision**. Go back to your story and look for possible ways to strengthen your characterization, plot, pacing, point of view, and

narration, based on your reading of the various techniques that make up a best-selling novel today.

Also, check for continuity, logistics, and time sequencing. Does your basic premise make sense? If the problem or dilemma your whole novel is based on is easily solved, you've got work to do. Go through the whole story and revise as you go. Always save the original copies first, in case you want to go back and incorporate paragraphs or scenes from them.

5. **Distance yourself.** Put your story aside for a few weeks and concentrate on other things. Then you'll have the distance to approach it with fresh eyes, as a reader.

6. **Now go through it as a potential reader (or an editor).** Change the font and print it up. Or send it to your e-reader or tablet. Then be sure to read it in a different location from where you wrote it. With pen in hand, mark it all up.

7. **Second revision.** Now go back and make the changes you noted while reading.

8. **Send it to beta readers,** about 3-6 volunteers – savvy, avid readers who enjoy your genre. See the list of specific questions in the previous chapter.

9. **Third revision.** Read through the feedback from your beta readers and seriously consider revising any parts that confused or bored them. Any areas of confusion or other issues mentioned by two or more of your readers should be red flags for you. Revise based on their suggestions.

10. **Professional Edit.** Now find a reputable freelance fiction editor who reads and edits your genre. Be sure to check out their website carefully and get a sample edit. Then a good idea is to contract them for the first 2-6 chapters to see how it goes before committing to a whole manuscript.

11. **Final revisions based on the edit.** Read your story out loud or use text-to-speech software to have it read aloud to you. This will

help you pick up on any awkward phrasing or anywhere that the flow is less than smooth. If you stumble over a sentence or have to read it again, revise it for easier flow. (Do this at any stage of your story.)

Also, either before the professional edit or after, try changing the double-spacing to single-spacing and the size to 6" x 9" (e-reader size) and sending your story to your Kindle or other e-reader. Then read it on there, as a reader rather than a writer, but with a notebook beside you. Or get a sample copy printed up as a book.

At this stage, be sure to read it in a different location from where you wrote it, to fool your brain into thinking that you're now a reader, instead of the writer.

12. **Get a final proofread of it**, if you can afford this step, or perhaps you've made arrangements for your copyeditor to do another, final pass to go over your revisions, looking for any new errors that may have cropped up as a result of your changes. (I edit in sections, and each section goes back and forth with the author at least two or three times.)

Now your story should be ready to send to agents and acquiring editors or to publish yourself. Good luck with it!

# APPENDICES

# Appendix 1 – Spot the POV Gaffes

Can you find the viewpoint (POV) errors in the examples below? (Answers at the end.)

1. A suspense-mystery:

Cartwright and his partner hurried out of the bar, hopped into the squad car, and sped off. They didn't notice a lean wiry man in a raincoat follow them out of the bar. He watched them drive away, then sprinted to his car.

2. A bad guy is looking for a critical file in someone's home. He doesn't know the family at all except for the name of the husband and father, whose office he's searching.

As he inspected the room, he carefully searched through desk drawers and flipped through files in the file cabinet. Before checking the computer, he picked up a framed picture of Jeannine and little Cody and studied it, then put it back exactly where he'd found it.

3. Janice hurried into the newsroom, where reporters were standing around, checking their phones and drinking stale coffee.

4. The waiter brought two glasses of water and the menus, and took their drink order. As they looked through the menus, Craig glanced surreptitiously at Michelle. Her face looked pinched and her knee jiggled quietly under the tablecloth.

5. Jocelyn got out of the pool, dripping wet, and flopped down on her beach blanket to dry off in the sun. Several men around her admired Jocelyn's curvy body and glowing, perfectly tanned skin as she lay face down by the pool, her eyes closed. Ahhh, this is the life, she thought. I need more vacations like this.

6. The bright sunlight shining through the bedroom window woke Steve up. He felt like crap. He had a splitting headache and there were big bags under his bloodshot eyes. Maybe if I go back to sleep, I'll wake up without a hangover. He turned away from the window and pulled the covers up.

7. Ellie got off the bus and headed toward her apartment, eager to get home and out of the cold. She couldn't wait to heat the leftovers and make a nice cup of tea. As she hurried along the dark street, she was unaware of the scruffy-looking man with a gun following her, getting closer and closer.

8. Joanne put down the phone then, frantic, called her husband Jake at work. "The school called and Jenny never showed up today! Where could she be?"

Jake excused himself from the meeting and went out into the hall, closing the door behind him. "What do you mean, she never showed up? Didn't she get on the bus this morning as usual?"

Joanne paced back and forth. "Yes, she did. So what could've happened to her?"

9. What the hell? How dare he? Charles felt like strangling the guy. A long throbbing vein snaked down Charles' forehead like a vine. He held his hands up as if he wanted to choke the reporter.

10. Nora cringed in the back seat of the car as the speeding Mercedes swerved, barely missing two young boys who were crossing the road. The two kids, relieved to still be alive, stared open-mouthed at the driver as he sped by. The driver was completely unconcerned. He never took his foot off the gas pedal as he continued to swerve and weave his way through the heavy traffic, determined to catch up to the car ahead. Nora clutched the handle above the window for dear life, trying to keep from being thrown across the rear seat.

11. The doorbell rang and Ruth hurried downstairs, calling, "Come in."

A thin, middle-aged woman with graying hair walked in and took off her brown coat, then smiled at Ruth. "Hi, honey."

"Hi, Mom," Ruth said. "Thanks for looking after the kids for a few hours."

12. This is the opening chapter of a middle-grade novel and Jeremy is the main character, so we should be in his head.

"I am not crazy," a slender boy named Jeremy Rogers shouted at the crowd of other fifth graders as they taunted him. His T-shirt had come untucked from the fight, exposing his bare back.

13. This is the beginning of a chapter of a spy story. Raymond is the good guy and the POV character for the chapter:

Raymond Morrison was the last to arrive. He watched from his car as the others arrived and headed through the pub and up to the room for the meeting. The suite was sparsely furnished and musty, with faded curtains and a layer of dust. A nearby building blocked the last rays of daylight, throwing the roadside inn into early twilight. No one turned on the lamp. Finally, Raymond got out and crossed the street, then navigated through the pub, ignoring his thirst, and hit the stairs. At the top, he found room 12 and knocked on the door.

# POV GAFFES REVEALED

1. We're in Cartwright's point of view, and he didn't see the man follow them and watch them drive away, so it shouldn't be worded like this in a scene in Cartwright's POV. Show this in another way, as in having Cartwright look in his rearview mirror and catch a glimpse of the guy and wonder about him or mention it to his partner.

2. The bad guy only knows the name of the husband/father – he doesn't know the names of the guy's kids. We know their names from previous scenes, so it's easy to let this little POV error slip in unnoticed. Instead, say "the guy's two kids" or whatever.

3. Janice just walked in, so how does she know the coffee is stale? Maybe say something like "drinking coffee – no doubt cold and stale, as usual."

4. We're in Craig's POV. How does he know Michelle's knee is jiggling quietly under the table?

5. Jocelyn is lying face down, so how does she know several men are admiring her body?

6. Steve can't see his bloodshot eyes or the bags under them. Wait until he looks in the bathroom mirror to comment on that.

7. Ellie is unaware of the scruffy-looking man following her, so this shouldn't be mentioned when we're in her point of view. Instead, have her catch a glimpse of him or hear approaching footsteps, and show her fear, wondering who could be following her, and why.

8. It's unlikely Joanne would know Jake is going out into the hall, unless he actually tells her, or she overhears him excusing himself from the meeting.

9. Charles can't see the bulging vein in his forehead. Show his fury from the inside, not as others would perceive from the outside.

10. How does Nora know how the kids are feeling? Maybe have her turning to see them staring open-mouthed. And as for the driver, you could say he "looked completely unconcerned" as she doesn't know exactly how he's feeling.

11. Ruth isn't thinking of her own mother as "a thin, middle-aged woman with graying hair." Just say "Her mother walked in." Then you could have Ruth commenting to her mother about her brown coat or coloring her gray hair or that she's looking thin, to show her mother's appearance.

12. We're in Jeremy's head, so he's not thinking of himself as "a slender boy named...." Also, he doesn't necessarily know that his bare back is exposed. You could have him wondering if it is, if that's relevant.

13. We're in Raymond's point of view and he's the last person to enter the room, but we get a description of the room while Raymond's still outside, in his car. Move the description of the room to after he enters it.

# Appendix 2 – What's in a Name? Naming Your Characters

Have you ever read a book where the name of the main character was jarring to you, seemed inappropriate, or just wrong? Or have you mixed up two characters because their names were similar? Or said "Who's that?" because suddenly the author started using a character's nickname or first name, when previously all you knew was their last name? What you choose to name your characters can be the difference between annoying or confusing your readers and having the story flow naturally, with all the little details falling into place to make a seamless, believable story world.

Several years ago, I did a critique of a novel in which the cruel, abusive father was named "Danny" and his eight-year-old abused son was named "John." I definitely thought "Danny" sounded much more like a nice kid than a nasty adult, and why not give the young boy a more kid-like name, like "Johnny"? Switching the two names would have worked fine, too.

**Here are some tips for naming your characters**:

~ Avoid too-common and too-forgettable names like "Jim," "John," "Bill Smith," or "Bob Jones."

~ Avoid really weird, unusual names that draw attention to themselves – unless it's for a really weird character!

~ Choose a name that fits the character's personality and role. Don't name your he-man hero "Harold" or "Wilfred," or your nasty, despicable villain "David" or "Josh" or "Matt" or "Richard" or "Jason" or "Matt" or any other very popular name. People don't want a nasty bad guy to have the same name as their brother, boyfriend, husband or son.

213

~ And of course avoid old-fashioned names for contemporary characters, like "Ebenezer" or "Cuthbert" or "Harold" or "Gertrude" or "Henrietta" or "Josephine."

~ Also, to reflect the actual makeup of North American society, be sure to use some characters and names from other ethnic backgrounds besides Anglo-Saxon.

~ If you're writing historical fiction, research common names for that era and location. Don't make the mistake of calling your 18th-century heroine, for example, "Taylor," which was used only for males in that era.

~ Even for contemporary fiction, don't name your 50- or 60-something male Jordan or Brandon or Justin or Tyler or Kyle, as those names weren't popular for babies 50 or 60 years ago. There are several websites where you can find the most popular baby names for any given year. For example, you can go to sheknows.com and type in the year to see a list of popular baby names for that year. For example, if your male character is 55, here are some of the most popular names for boys in 1960: David, Michael, James, John, Robert, Mark, William, Richard, and Thomas. If you've got a 23-year old male, some of the most popular baby names for boys in 1992 were: Michael, Christopher, Andrew, Matthew, Joshua, Brandon, Tyler, Ryan, Zachary, Justin, and Kyle.

From typing in the year of birth on the same website, here are some popular names for a 19-year-old girl, born in 1996: Jessica, Ashley, Taylor, Samantha, Alexis, Sarah, Megan, Amanda, and Stephanie. For your 28-year-old spunky, savvy heroine, some popular names for girls born in 1987 were: Jessica, Ashley, Amanda, Jennifer, Sarah, Stephanie, Brittany, Nicole, Megan, Melissa, and Danielle. For a 63-year-old woman, Linda, Patricia, Nancy, Karen, Barbara, Susan, Deborah, Carol, Sandra, Donna and Sharon were all very popular names in 1952. And an 83-year-old woman born in 1932 might be named Mary, Betty, Norma, Doris, Helen, Mildred, Dorothy, Joan, Ruth, Shirley, or Alice, among other possibilities.

~ Don't confuse your readers by naming different characters in the same story similar names, like two guys named Jason and Jake, or two women named Eileen and Ellie. In fact, it's best to avoid using the same first letter for different characters' names in the same book, like Damian and David, or even similar internal sounds, like Janice and Alice or Helen" and Elsie. You can help the readers out even more by varying the number of syllables of your main characters' names.

~ Be flexible about the names you choose. As your story and characters develop, you may decide to rename some of them to suit new character traits they've taken on. Then you can use your "Find and Replace" function to change the name throughout the whole manuscript in seconds.

~ Finally, what about characters who are called different names by different people? That can get confusing for readers who are barreling along trying to keep up with your fast-paced plot. Suppose you have a female police officer named Caroline Hunter. The other officers call her "Hunter" at work, her friends call her "Caroline" and her family calls her "Carrie." It would be unrealistic to have her friends and family call her "Hunter" just to help the readers out. So, as a reminder, be sure to throw in her full name from time to time, like during introductions or whatever. Also, if you start a scene using "Hunter," it's best to avoid switching to "Caroline," as the inattentive reader might suddenly wonder who this Caroline is who just walked in. Keep "Hunter" for that scene, with perhaps the occasional use of her full name. If she's with her parents and sister, she'll be "Carrie" but you could throw in the "Caroline" or "Hunter" somewhere, as a reminder, like when she's answering the phone, or when a neighbor kid addresses her mom as "Mrs. Hunter."

As you're searching names, make lists of names and nicknames that appeal to you for future writing, under different categories, such as hero, heroine, male villain, female villain, best friend, boss mother, and father.

# Appendix 3 – Sketching in Your Characters

As you formulate the plot and main characters of your novel, start jotting down info on your protagonist and other important characters, and keep filling it in as ideas occur to you. This way, you can get to know them so well that, when they're thrown into the thick of the action or interacting with others, you won't need to wonder how they'd act or what they'd say in various situations – you'll already have a good handle on their background, personality, strengths, weaknesses, preferences, fears, and goals in life. Readers are quick to judge if they think a fictional person is acting "out of character" or inconsistent with their upbringing or personality.

Here's a checklist to guide you in brainstorming and creating your main character's personality and background. Of course, their habits will need to fit their personality profile – a careful, precise person wouldn't have a messy office, for example.

Most of this information won't appear in your story, and the details that do should just be mentioned in passing in natural ways that fit seamlessly into the scene, without the author intruding to fill in the readers on detailed character background info.

**The Basics:**

~ Name – and as you go along, does it still fit the character? If not, you can always change it later, as you get to know him/her better.

~ Gender, age and education

~ Occupation/Profession, and how they feel about it

~ Physical attributes: Maybe find a photo online or in a magazine that best represents your protagonist, and keep it handy it as a quick reference. Also, how they feel about their height, weight, hair, etc.

## Background:

~ Where they grew up. Characters raised in the Deep South, the Ozark Mountains, Idaho, California, Montana and New York City will all be quite different.

~ Socio-economic status of their family as they were growing up. Were they struggling, middle-class, or privileged?

~ Family background: Fifth-generation established or immigrant blue-collar parents? Happy or unhappy family life? Only child or lots of siblings? Loving or absentee parents? Sibling rivalry? Adopted? Orphaned?

~ Was there alcoholism, abuse, or incest in their childhood? Or other family shames or secrets?

~ Highlights from childhood: Anything that stands out that has affected them, either positively or negatively.

~ Past significant relationships or marriage(s), and how they affect their present outlook.

## Personality and character:

~ Personality: outgoing or shy, lighthearted or serious, tactful or outspoken, laid-back or hyper/workaholic, neat or messy, and so on. Also, any interesting personality quirks.

~ Hopes, dreams, goals: What does this character really want in life?

~ Strengths and talents: What is he or she most proud of?

~ Any strong feelings or attitude(s) toward causes, people, politics, etc.

~ Insecurities and perceived weaknesses – maybe they grew up in a rural area and feel out of their element in the city, or wish they could cook or dance better, or were fitter or more outgoing.

~ Any other points of vulnerability, flaws, or weaknesses that work against them

~ Biggest fears, phobias, and disappointments, especially secret ones

~ Biggest "baggage" to date – shameful secrets or unresolved problems and issues from the past that still affect their attitudes and reactions today

~ What others think of this character

~ Other significant people in their life: best friends, close family members, and other supporting characters, and their role in relationship to protagonist

~ Any enemies or irritating acquaintances

~ Significant interests, hobbies, strong likes and dislikes

**Their surroundings:**

~ A description of his or her current living and working conditions – home, workplace. Neat or messy? Sparse or cluttered? Elegant or thrown together?

~ Most treasured possessions, and why?

Now you should have a good handle on your main character, so you'll be able to quickly decide how he would react in any given situation the antagonist and events throw at him. As you're writing, you may find this character's personality is changing, or you might think of more interests, strengths, phobias, or personality quirks – just add/change them to your character sketch as you go along.

# Thank you!

Thanks for reading *Captivate Your Readers*. I hope you found it helpful for creating, writing, and revising your fiction.

If you'd like to know when my next books are available and also about blog posts, sales, contests, and free offers, you can sign up for my newsletter at my blog or one of my websites, www.JodieRenner.com or www.JodieRennerEditing.com.

Reviews help other readers find books. I appreciate you taking a minute to leave a quick review on Amazon.com or wherever you purchased this book. Even a line or two would be great. Even if you got this book out of the library or at a conference or bookstore, you can still leave a review on Amazon.com.

You've just read the third full-length book in the series, *An Editor's Guide to Writing Compelling Fiction*. The other books in the series are the multi-award-winning *Fire up Your Fiction* and *Writing a Killer Thriller*. You can read the Introduction and first few chapters of each of them on Amazon.

All three books are available in both e-book and trade paperback form. The paperback versions are in many public libraries and independent bookstores. I hope you enjoy them all!

# Acknowledgments

I'd like to thank my eagle-eyed, insightful beta readers, Tom Combs, Robert Beatty, Steve Hooley, Iola Goulton, Victoria Ichizli-Bartels, Sylvia Ney, Dale Smith, Alex Fenton, Mark Wayne Adams, and Lynn Sholes.

This is the first time I've used beta readers, and they all volunteered after a mention by me on Facebook and in a comment under a blog post on *The Kill Zone* blog, where I post on alternate Mondays. I'm so grateful they all offered to have a look at my earlier versions.

I'd also like to thank Chris Pepples, who copyedited many of the chapters.

And thanks to my good friend John Kurtze, who suggested this title.

# Other Books by Jodie Renner

**FIRE UP YOUR FICTION**
**An Editor's Guide to Writing Compelling Stories**

ISBN: 978-0993700408

If you're looking to hone your style, bring your scenes to life, tighten your writing, add tension, pick up the pace, and develop a more authentic, appealing voice, this multi-award-winning guide to the indispensable style elements of writing a popular novel is for you.

"This should be on the booklist for Master's Programs in Writing for Publication."

~ Judge, Writer's Digest Contest

"This book is packed with good advice on how to spot and fix weaknesses in your fiction writing. It summarizes the combined wisdom of the last century or so of fiction teachers into one handy volume."

~ Randy Ingermanson, bestselling author of *Writing Fiction For Dummies*

"A handy checklist and self-editing guide that will get any fiction writer to a stronger, well-told tale."

~ James Scott Bell, bestselling author of *Revision & Self-Editing, Plot & Structure*, and more

"*Fire up Your Fiction* is the Strunk and White for writers who want to be not just mere storytellers but master story-compellers."
~ IndieReader review

**WRITING A KILLER THRILLER**
**An Editor's Guide to Writing Compelling Fiction**

ISBNs (2 editions): 978-1490389943 and 978-0993700422

Respected editor Jodie Renner offers indispensable advice for creating fast-paced, compelling fiction. Both published and aspiring authors of suspense-thrillers and other popular fiction will find these tips indispensable for plotting your story, creating compelling characters, writing a gripping opening, designing suspenseful scenes, picking up the pace, ramping up the tension and intrigue, revising for power, and creating a page-turner that sells.

"Finally, someone who understands the thriller! More than ever, an author must also be his own best editor, and Jodie Renner is there to help. *Writing a Killer Thriller* should be on every thriller writer's desk. It breaks down the thriller into its must-have component parts to write a scintillating, edge-of-the-seat novel that will get readers buzzing and sales flowing."

~ ROBERT DUGONI, New York Times bestselling author of *The Jury Master, Murder One,* and *My Sister's Grave*

"Writing is hard, editing harder, and self-editing almost impossible. *Writing a Killer Thriller* demystifies each of these steps on the road to a published manuscript. Read this book. It will help you now and for many years to come."

~ DP LYLE, award-winning author of many nonfiction and fiction books

## QUICK CLICKS: WORD USAGE
### Precise Word Choices at Your Fingertips

This quick and easy, reliable e-reference to current word usage and style answers all those questions and many more. It's a user-friendly, time-saving guide to the most appropriate words and usage for every level of English communication.

Writers, journalists, students, teachers, bloggers, copy editors, proofreaders, small business owners, academics, and anyone with a writing project on the go will love this clickable e-reference with all its internal links.

## QUICK CLICKS: SPELLING LIST
### Commonly Misspelled Words at Your Fingertips

This time-saving writers' resource by sought-after book editor Jodie Renner is a clickable list of words and phrases that, for one reason or another, often trip up even good spellers and slow down their work. By using this handy alphabetical spelling glossary with lots of links, you can find answers fast and get back to what really matters – your message and content.

Whether you're a journalist, fiction or nonfiction writer, student, teacher, blogger, editor, or anyone else on a busy schedule (aren't we all these days?), this clickable spelling list will save you tons of time.

# About the Author

Jodie Renner, a former English teacher with a master's degree, is a sought-after freelance fiction editor and award-winning author of two other craft-of-writing guides to date. *Fire up Your Fiction* has won two silver medals (Readers' Favorite Awards, 2014, FAPA President's Book Awards, 2013), and an Honorable Mention in Writer's Digest E-Book Awards for 2013. Jodie's *Writing a Killer Thriller* is also valued by fiction writers of all genres who want to engage readers by adding tension, suspense, and intrigue to their novel.

Jodie is also a well-known blogger, and her craft-of-writing articles and other resources for writers appear on various blogs, including her group blog, *The Kill Zone* (alternate Mondays) and occasionally on her own blog, *Resources for Writers*.

Jodie presents workshops at writers' conferences and to writers' groups across North America. See JodieRenner.com/workshops for more details. She also judges novels and short stories for various organizations, including several times for Writer's Digest.

When she's not editing, writing, or reading novels or books on writing compelling fiction, Jodie loves to pursue her two other passions, photography and traveling. She has traveled extensively throughout North America, Europe and the Middle East, and continues to sneak away whenever she gets the chance.

# RESOURCES & PERMISSIONS

## Resources

James Scott Bell, *Revision & Self-Editing*

Jack M. Bickham, *The 38 Most Common Fiction Writing Mistakes (And How to Avoid Them)*

Anthony Brown and Darrin English, *Stickman Review*

Sally Carpenter, "Overwriting – Less is More" in Five Scribes blog

Miriam Darnell, "Creating an Interesting Bad Guy"

Randy Ingermanson & Peter Economy, *Writing Fiction for Dummies*

Steven James, *Story Trumps Structure*

Mary Kole "Two Signs of Overwriting and Why It's a Problem"

Elizabeth Lyon, *A Writer's Guide to Fiction*

Donald Maass, *Writing the Breakout Novel*

Donald Maass, *The Fire in Fiction*

Jessica Page Morrell, *Thanks, But This Isn't For Us*

David Morrell, *The Successful Novelist*

Sol Stein, *How to Grow a Novel*

William Strunk, Jr. and E.B. White, *The Elements of Style*

Chuck Wendig, "25 Things You Should Know About Antagonists"

## Permissions

Permission has been granted from:

HarperCollins for excerpts from *Moonlight Mile* by Dennis Lehane

Tom Combs for excerpts from his novel, *Nerve Damage*

Think of ~~one of your~~ friends (real). ~~ Y~~ ... not Give
the person a fictitious name.

Where did yr meet that person, Ⓑ under what
How was that person dressed? Circum? Occasion?

What was your first impression of him/her

Of the two of yr, who spoke first & what
did you/he/she say?

What was his/her/ your reply?

What attitude did the person's body language suggest?

Would you ...

... It ... what
will yr ...